The Best of
SOUTHWOLD

The lighthouse in Southwold was built in 1892. There are 112 steps
up to the lantern.

The Best of
SOUTHWOLD

EDITED BY
JOHN MILLER

FOREWORD BY
Michael Palin

SUTTON PUBLISHING
ADNAMS AND COMPANY PLC

This book is dedicated to the memory of Derek Hall, author,
journalist and a great friend, who lived in Ferry Road and
loved Southwold.

First published in the United Kingdom in 1998 by
Sutton Publishing Limited · Phoenix Mill
Thrupp · Stroud · Gloucestershire · GL5 2BU
in association with Adnams Sole Bay Brewery,
Southwold, Suffolk, IP18 6JW

Reprinted 1998 (twice), 2000

British Library Cataloguing in Publication Data
A catalogue record for this book is available from the British Library

ISBN 0 7509 1864 0

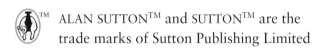 ALAN SUTTON™ and SUTTON™ are the
trade marks of Sutton Publishing Limited

Typeset in 11/18pt Sabon
Typesetting and origination by
Sutton Publishing Limited
Printed in Great Britain by
J.H. Haynes & Co., Sparkford.

CONTENTS

CONTENTS

CONTENTS

CONTENTS

FOREWORD

I first set foot in Southwold in the summer of 1958. My father, methodical and conservative in all things, had a sudden rush of blood to the head and decided that after years of summer holidays in Sheringham in Norfolk it was time for a change. I was fifteen years old and am ashamed to say that despite a Geography 'O' level had never heard of the place. I felt we were moving somewhere as remote and exotic as Samarkand.

Little did I know then that over the next thirty-two years Southwold would become an indelible part of my life.

During our second year there I met my future wife, on the beach in front of our regular summer quarters, Glan-Y-Don guest house. In 1966 my parents left Sheffield for good and retired to nearby Reydon. In 1969 some of the first episodes of *Monty Python* were filmed in and around the town – I pushed John Cleese off the harbour wall while he was sitting at a desk reading the news. After my father's death in 1977 my mother moved to a flat in Southwold overlooking The Common, in which she died in 1990.

In all that time, as my life changed around me, Southwold remained the same. I never once tired of coming down from London, either in the clattering swaying diesel train from Ipswich or later, when my mother could no longer drive, along the A12 as it shed cities and towns and began to follow the sea.

Arriving at Darsham station or turning off along the road that led only to Southwold never ceased to create a sense of heightened expectancy, a special and enticing feeling of branching off from the mainstream.

Southwold remains largely untouched by the march of progress. By which I certainly do not mean it is any way backward. Quite the opposite. It seems to have an entirely healthy attitude to progress which is that a little goes a long way.

Southwold has facilities that would grace a much bigger town. It has two fine hotels of great character, restaurants, greens, a common, a brewery, a lighthouse, a theatre and an imposing medieval church. You can walk around the lot in less than an hour and yet it never feels small.

It has always seemed to me to be a town at ease with itself. (I could be wrong. For all I know, Council meetings might be like feeding time at the zoo.) It quietly, but firmly, resists bumptious outsiders. Aggrandizement is not in its nature. Development is tolerated but discouraged. This is not because of any meanness of spirit, lack of generosity or simple Nimbyism. The fact is that Southwold is not a place anyone in their right mind would want to change.

The civility of the people, the harmony of the streets and houses, and the harmony of the whole with the countryside around it – wild and protective at the same time – is something rare these days. As is its rejection of the twee and phoney. Southwold is a working town, not at all comfortable with being called pretty. It is a settled, civilized enclave, surrounded by sea, marsh, river and an indefinable air of mystery. This is perhaps what sends so many of us potty about the place, and I suspect, sends many more on up the A12 in search of more immediate rewards.

Nearly forty years after I first crunched my painful way across the shingle beach looking for somewhere to plant my cricket stumps, savagely cursing my father for taking me away from the wide, firm, acres of Sheringham sand, I have never found anywhere in the world with the same appeal.

I have come to accept that the day my father chose Southwold was the day he changed my life.

MICHAEL PALIN

1997

ACKNOWLEDGEMENTS

Having amassed thousands of words written about Southwold in newspapers, magazines and books, I decided a few years ago to turn them into a talk to entertain local societies. It was entitled 'As others see us' and later, 'Is it true what they say about Southwold?' – the genesis of this book. Thus I am grateful to all those audiences who enjoyed the talks and encouraged me to put under the microscope the life and times of our extraordinary large village by the sea in which we are so lucky to live.

Several residents deserve special thanks for their help and advice: Berta Browett and David Lee who run the Southwold Archaeological and Natural History Society's museum in Victoria Street, Geraldine Bryant, Dudley Clarke, Susannah Collings, Harold Kemp, Kay Kiddy, Beattie King, Rachel Lawrence, Ann Lawson, John Purdy and Ann Thornton. I am also indebted to those who personally gave permission to reproduce their work – Miles Kington, Margot Strickland, Byron Rogers, Cal McCrystal, Steve Boggan, Maureen Lipman, Dr Peter Sager, Terry Reeve and George Bumstead. And I have since become a big fan of Michael Palin, another Southwold enthusiast, who wrote the foreword to the book while in the throes of creating another hugely successful BBC travel programme.

I also thank the Southwold and Reydon Society, the Suffolk Preservation Society, *Punch*, *Independent* Newspaper Publishing, the *Evening Standard*, *Suffolk-Norfolk Life*, the *Good Housekeeping* helpline, the *Lowestoft Journal*, Helen Surtees and Dr Piers Mackesy, for permitting me to use pieces of which they owned copyright. Although unlikely, it is just possible that I have failed to track down owners of work still in copyright, but I hope that if they see how their words have been revived in a beautifully produced, highly readable book, they will forgive me. A few small changes have been made to some of the pieces for reasons of brevity, clarity and anonymity.

Simon Loftus, chairman of Adnams and Company Plc and who knows a thing or two about both wine and words was enthusiastic and encouraging about this anthology. I am very grateful to Adnams, very much the heartbeat of Southwold, for making a valuable contribution to the book's publication.

The Best of Southwold contains some delightful photographs. Some of these have come from the archives of Southwold Town Council and I would like to thank Jenny Hursell, the Clerk, and Councillors Ros McDermott and John Winter for their help. The contemporary pictures are the work of two fine photographers. One is Stephen Wolfenden who was responsible for the picture on the jacket and other photographs, and also let me use work from his remarkable photographic essay, 'To the Town: Portraits of Southwold'. The other is Richard Wells who is building a considerable picture library of Southwold and its happenings.

And last, but decidedly not least, my thanks go to my most valued critic, my wife Brenda, for her guidance and encouragement.

Fishermen's huts along the North Cliff at the turn of the century.

In the Reign of
King Edward VII

Southwold in the opening years of the twentieth century and the coronation year of King Edward VII is one of the brightest, prettiest and quaintest little seaside towns in England and one of the very healthiest and most beneficial sanitary resorts in the whole United Kingdom. It lies off the beaten track, 'far from the madding crowd', and forms no stage or junction on any of the great highways of the world, by which its name might become familiar to the travelling public, and it is unknown to the roving tramps, minstrels and mountebanks who infest the great thoroughfares of the kingdom.

It is not a rendezvous even for the genial but undesirable tripper whose frolics enliven most of our popular holiday resorts, and it makes no effort to attract visitors by misleading and extravagant advertisement of miraculous medicinal springs or association past or present with the famous leaders of fashionable society. Nevertheless Southwold has its own charms and it may be confidently asserted that those who have once enjoyed the good fortune of spending a holiday in this delightful little seaside retreat will marvel how such unrivalled charms should remain so long unknown and unappreciated, or how such exquisite rural beauties can have been preserved in the twentieth century when all the rest of the world seems overrun and vulgarised with the noise, bustle and traffic of modern life and enterprise.

Southwold in fact is a typical survival of old-fashioned English rural scenery in a typical corner of East Anglia – a district that now constitutes one of the most exquisite of the few surviving remnants of quaint, beautiful old-world England, the England of the good old times, the historic idyllic old England we

Holidaymakers enjoy the Southwold sunshine below Gun Hill shortly before the start of the First World War. The bathing machines on the right were moved in and out of the sea according to the tides.

have all imagined in our youthful dreams and loved in the yearnings of our romantic childhood. Not indeed that the imagination of any modern city child, or adult, can conjure up a picture in any degree approaching the living reality.

Southwold, with its delightful old village greens, its purple heaths and spacious commons, its picturesque cliffs and creeks and ferries, its refulgent sunsets lighting up the marshes with an ineffable glow of golden tints, and its superb outlook over the great blue majestic and limitless ocean. Southwold, bathed in perennial sunshine, surrounded by matchless scenery and sanctified by its wonderful old-world traditions and associations is far too singular in its characteristics to present itself to the imagination of even the most poetic dreamer whose experiences have been confined to the pent-up cities and beaten tracks of the prosaic modern world.

To the city dweller it is a new world, a veritable Eden, whose pure, fragrant ozone-laden atmosphere and genial reposeful homeliness afford as surprising a contrast to their usual environment as light to darkness or joyous youth to oppressed and irritable old age.

SOUTHWOLD AND NEIGHBOURHOOD
1900

Swallows

DANIEL DEFOE

From Dunwich we come to Swole, or Southole. This is a small port town upon the coast at the mouth of a little river called the Blith. I found no business the people here were employed in but the fishery for herrings and sprats which they cure by the help of smoke as they do at Yarmouth.

There is but one church in this town but it is a very large one and well built, as most of the churches in this county are, and of impenetrable flint. Indeed there is no occasion for its being so large, for staying there on Sabbath Day I was surprised to see an extraordinary large church, capable of receiving five or six thousand people and but 27 in it besides the parson and clerk: but at the same time the meeting-house of dissenters was full to the very doors, having, as I guessed, from six to 800 people in it.

This town is made famous for a very great engagement at sea, in the year 1672, between the English and Dutch fleets, in the bay opposite to the town in which, not to be partial to ourselves, the English fleet was worsted and the brave Montague, Earl of Sandwich, Admiral under the Duke of York, lost his life. The ship *Royal Prince* carrying 100 guns in which he was and which was under him, commanded by Sir Edward Spragg, was burnt and several other ships lost, and about 600 seamen: part of those killed in the fight were, as I was told, brought on shore here and buried in the churchyard of this town, as others also were at Ipswich.

The guardship at North Parade in 1897. Five coastguards are on duty.

At this town in particular . . . is the ordinary place where our summer friends, the swallows, first land when they come to visit us, and here they may be said to embark for their return when they go back into warmer climates, and as I think the following remark though of so trifling a circumstance, may be both instructing as well as diverting, it may be very proper in this place.

I was some years before at this place, at the later end of the year, viz. October, and lodging in a house that looked into the churchyard, I observed in the evening an unusual multitude of birds sitting on the leads of the church. Curiosity led me to go nearer to see what they were and I found they were all swallows, that there was such an infinite number that they covered the whole roof of the church and of several houses near and perhaps might of more houses which I did not see. This led me to enquire of a grave gentlemen whom I saw near me, what the meaning was of such a prodigious multitude of swallows sitting there.

'O sir,' he says, turning towards the sea, 'you may see the reason, the wind is off the sea.'

I did not seem fully informed by that expression, so he goes on: 'I perceive, Sir,' says he, 'you are a stranger to it. You must then understand first that this is the season of the year when the swallows, their food here failing, begin to leave us and return to the country, wherever it be, from whence, I suppose they came. And this being the nearest to the coast of Holland they come here to embark.'

This he said, smiling a little, 'And now, Sir,' says he, 'the weather being too calm, or the wind contrary, they are waiting for a gale, for they are all wind-bound.'

This was more evident to me when in the morning I found the wind had come about to the north-west in the night, and there was not one swallow to be seen, of near a million, which I believe was there the night before.

How those creatures know that this part of the Island of Great Britain is the way to their home, or the way that they are to go, that this very point is the nearest way over, or even that the nearest cut is before them, that we must leave to the naturalists to determine who insist upon it that brutes cannot think.

TOUR THROUGH THE EASTERN COUNTIES
1724

Far-away places have nothing on Southwold

MILES KINGTON

There is a certain travel writer who writes for a certain newspaper about the exotic places he goes to who is without doubt the most boring and characterless journalist in the world today. Mauritius, Hong Kong, the

Seychelles, China – he makes them all sound as exciting as a bus ride along Oxford Street. I wouldn't be surprised to find that after he has written a place up its tourist trade drops dramatically.

I can't get to Mauritius. It's not so much the shortage of money, though that helps. It's the shortage of time caused by the fact that we go on holiday every year for two weeks to the same place up the Suffolk coast. The family has been going there every year for fifteen years or more. When we first went there we were carrying the children in little carry-cots, now the children are carrying my bags for me.

And every year, as they get bigger and bigger, I say to them: 'Well, children. Is it to be Mauritius this year for a change?' And every year they say: 'Not on your life – we've got to go back to Southwold!'

It's the sort of place that what's-his-name never writes about. It's the sort of holiday that *nobody* ever seems to write about. Travel features always have to be about far-off, colourful places with souks, casbahs and market places – Sri Lanka, Peru, Indonesia. Who'd want to write about a little town in East Anglia, accessible only via the exotic A12?

Me, that's who. There's just a chance that next year the children might want to go abroad for a change, and I'd like to get down in writing, before I forget, the fact that it is still, even in 1982, possible to have a family seaside holiday, and enjoy it.

One of the nice things about going back to the same place year after year is seeing how little things change. And I don't mean that we rush down to the beach and shout, 'Hallo shingle! Hallo sands!' Actually the beach changes dramatically every year. The town builds new breakwaters now and then (the children prefer to call them groynes: anything with an overtone of sex still causes hilarity) and every year the sea covers them up with a new coating of shingle.

No, it's the family next door we rush to have a look at. Our rented flat overlooks several gardens and one of them contains the grossest family you ever saw. When they were babies they cried all the time. Last year they spent

In Southwold the Roman ceremony of beating the bounds is held intermittently over a four-and-a-half-mile route. The boundaries of the parish are traced out, and certain points are beaten with rods.

all their time hitting the family dog, a huge friendly spaniel. This winter he will probably bite them because this summer they had graduated to hitting each other. It's a team effort because child A holds child B so that child C can kick the living daylights out of it. Then they swap roles and start again. Gross.

Great theatre though. Actually the town has its own theatre, or at least the church hall is taken over every summer by a troupe of actors who for eight or ten weeks put on a new play every week. You can guess what sort of stuff. A thriller, an Agatha Christie, a sparkling comedy, an Ayckbourn, a Douglas Home. . . . They change the plays on Thursday. Clever that. If you're there for a week you can go to two plays, for a fortnight, three plays and so on. Over the High Street during the season flies a banner reading 'SOUTHWOLD SUMMER THEATRE' and if you look very carefully you can read the faded words, Frinton Summer Theatre, which is where the company was fourteen years ago but they obviously prefer Southwold, and who wouldn't?

It's one of the prettiest towns you could image. No, pretty is the wrong word. Handsome is more like it. Lots of attractive houses built from a warm red-orange brick. Lots of open greens, a white lighthouse right in the middle of town, an old-fashioned brewery with old-fashioned drays drawn by horses, a great big flinty Suffolk church, flowers, pubs, wind, blue sky, the sea. And the best thing about it is that it's at the end of the road: you can't go through it to somewhere else, because it's built on a sort of landlocked island bounded by the harbour, The Common, the river and creek all round the town. And the sea.

Sounds groovy, eh? Of course, the embarrassing questions are, yes, but what do you actually *do*? Go on the beach and build sandcastles? Look at wild flowers? *Swim in the North Sea*?

Well, looking back, I can't particularly remember anything we've actually done in the last fifteen years. But then you don't *do* things in a place like that – you just *be* in a place like that. Like, for instance, the local bookshop hires out bikes (everyone does something else: you buy the theatre tickets in the local jewellery shop) and we generally hire bikes on the first day and go on bike rides when we're bored. Along the disused railway, through the woods and up the estuary, down to the harbour to buy crabs or anything else the fishermen have brought in, along the smugglers' paths in the marshes, along miles and miles of beach, falling off when you hit a soft bit and bicyling through the waves if you're brave.

There's always something happening down the harbour. This year they were putting a boring platform together to tow out to sea. There was a cargo ship registered in Panama. There were two boats that went aground just outside the harbour mouth. There was the 2nd British Crabbing Competition with hundreds of spectators, though it was hard to see what they could see as the crabs tend to be very small but at least you could buy a T-shirt saying 'I caught crabs at Walberswick'. Ha ha.

And if there's nothing happening at the harbour, there's the market. Not quite a casbah, at least I assume casbahs don't just happen on Thursday

Summer crowds gather in the market place to hear the Mayor's speech in 1997.

mornings, but good in its own way, especially the second-hand bookstall where I always go to browse and always come away with fifteen quids' worth of books. This year I got a rare Graham Greene, an interesting Evelyn Waugh travel book, a book about London pubs illustrated by Edward Ardizzone, and best of all a book about how Houdini did all his tricks.

Perhaps the best thing about Southwold though is the feeling that you're so far from London. This has its negative side. Shops close for lunch, and there's also a half-closing day. There's a notice in the Post Office suggesting that you should have mailed your letters yesterday if you want them to arrive. But the positive side far outweighs these minor distractions. People still trust each other, for instance. Nobody ever locks up their bikes, and often they leave shopping in their baskets. People in shops look at your bank card and wave it away as totally unnecessary. There's a little bookshop that leaves a rack of paperbacks outside overnight with a sign, 'Please put your money through the door if you buy a book'.

And these supposedly country bumpkins have got it right. One morning I was in Lloyds Bank waiting to cash a cheque and there was a bloke at the head of the queue, real poncey international English traveller, who had a bank account in France and wanted to pass one of his little froggy cheques. The conversation between him and the barely audible Suffolk burr behind the grille could not have been improved upon . . .

'What's the maximum amount of francs I can make the cheque out for?'

'Don't need to bother with francs, sterling is fine, 'ee just make it out for pounds . . .'

'But I've got to make it out in francs and there's an upper limit. Just tell me what the limit is.'

'Don't care about no limit, you just make it out in pounds, we'll cash anything . . .'

'Oh, for heaven's sake, don't you know anything about international banking?'

'Not a great deal, just make out a cheque and we'll give you some money . . .'

'Certainly not. I'm going to a bank where they know more about these things than you do. Goodbye!'

He stormed out and everyone in the bank burst into laughter. For one thing they knew there was only one other bank in the town and as one old man in the queue said. 'They don't know more there than what they do 'ere. 'E'll be back.' And the next old man in the queue said, 'Give me this cheque in fives and I don't want none of them francs if you don't mind.' It's not too hard to tell who looked like a bumpkin in all that. The international traveller. The bloke who probably reads all the travel features in magazines. God knows what he was doing in Southwold.

Of course it's not really a typical English town because it's quite well off and there are an awful lot of retired couples and they don't get hit by recessions (nor rewarded by booms). But it's still the best sort of holiday place around and I'm here today to tell you that sort of place still exists. Of course, I don't want you to actually go there. I want to keep it to myself. And I don't suppose my description of it has actually excited you to the point of wanting to go there. Which suits me fine. I just want to place on record the fact that I wouldn't swap it for anywhere else in the world. I have a terrible feeling that if the children go hitching to Mauritius next year I shall be going off to Southwold by myself.

MS LONDON
1982

A Day Out Like Your Mother Used to Make

STEVE BOGGAN

Eight a.m. in Southwold, Suffolk, and already it feels like 80 degrees. The town is waking up, busy by its standards, but to you, an outsider, one of the quietest places you have known. There is no sun, the clouds are heavy but only pale grey; it might rain – you hope it does because the day is already burnt out.

On the beach below the promenade, about 50 yards from the Sailors' Reading Room, a group of travellers, only slightly crusty, is stirring; four adults and two children, stretching and talking quietly next to the embers of their fire. The oldest child, aged about three, wants to swim. Two boys are flying kites nearby; a man is assembling a windsurfing board. The rest of the beach is deserted.

The presence of the travellers is to be discussed all day long in what is arguably Britain's most twee, nay *nice*, seaside town. They don't know this. They pack up and leave, tidying up their mess, two hours later.

But they have been noticed by a tiny population becoming increasingly sensitive to visitors, even though visitors of one type or another have been

Centre Cliff with its hotel in 1905. Much of the wide path was washed away
by storms in the following year.

their stock-in-trade for hundreds of years. There is something now that
grates among a section of the community that did not grate before.

Southwold, a once busy fishing harbour lying on the east coast between
Lowestoft to the north and Aldeburgh to the south, has been well and truly
discovered. Tourists – about 5,000 of them at any one time in the summer –
are wending their way noisily, coughing their cars along its quiet streets,
parking unceremoniously, enjoying themselves with neither guilt nor
apology, eating, drinking and all so joyously. So sickeningly *wholesomely*.

Southwold, population 1,700, is an historic settlement, the nearest port to
Amsterdam, a place peopled by hardy, friendly, resourceful men and women
with a sense of history and sufficient a grasp on the present to know they are
lucky to live where they do.

Most also know they are captured in a time warp. No noisy clubs here, no candyfloss, no big dippers, corkscrews, sick-making machinery; precious few arcade games or hungry fruit machines. Instead, holidays like your mother used to make.

You can make them now for your children. And it doesn't really matter whether they enjoy them, because you know you will. You will satiate your appetite for the simplicity of the past and you will tell yourself your children never had it so good. Nostalgia isn't what it used to be, but this is.

Eleven a.m. and in the Sailors' Reading Room one of the travellers is concentrating on the exhibits in the front section of the building. The room, a haven for the retired men of the town, was built in 1869 by a Mrs Rayley after the death of her husband, a master mariner.

The quiet, unwashed man shuffles from the model of the steamship *Glencona* to a five-foot schooner carved in the memory of George Parkyns

The High Street in 1921: not a motor vehicle in sight.

Ellis, 'Drowned by the upsetting of the Southwold lifeboat, February 27, 1858, aged 18'. He passes by the plate photograph of bygone fishermen like Sloper Hurr, Slummy Ashmanal and Brushy Watson, and walks out into the breaking sunshine.

In the partitioned rear of the room, reserved for members only, two retired bricklayers are playing snooker. They saw the travellers and their fire this morning but react with none of the rancour fellow citizens will display later today.

'The visitors who come here respect the place,' said one of the members. 'The people on the beach had a fire and they were boiling some water for their tea. It's a hell of a job. Good luck to them!'

Both men regret the loss of a number of grocers and bakers that were sold and turned into holiday homes. They regret also the increasing (although amazingly low) crime rate, the theft (twice) of the contents of the reading room's donations box: 'Once they brought back the empty box and once they took that too.'

But the tourists?

One of the members answers, 'If it wasn't for the visitors, this place would close down. We know that. Most of the people who come are no problem.'

So who does resent them?

'The outsiders. The people who come here, buy places and then want to keep it for themselves. All along Victoria Street used to be fishermen's cottages. Now they're owned by people who live in London.'

Nothing new here. Most villages in the country will tell you a similar story. But they don't have the added aggravation of thousands of visitors.

Lunch time. The daily inhabitants of Southwold's row of pastel-coloured beach huts (which sell at up to £8,000 each) are brewing up. Toothless retirees in coats and paisley headscarves are sucking potted beef rolls. Picnic gatherings are dotted along the shoreline between the rows of breakwaters vanishing into the brown sea. Tartan travel rugs, flasks, surprisingly large numbers of *white* sandwiches in Tupperware boxes. A low flesh : body ratio.

The beach is spacious and quiet. No ghetto-blasters, no seaside cafés spewing music. At the southern end of the parade, the front is pebbled, immaculately clean. The further north you go, the more sandy it becomes. Here, small games of cricket with tiny bats and tiny wickets are under way. Fathers are teaching their sons to play cover drives: girls are building sandcastles. You expect the George Bush campaign team to emerge from the waves and start talking *family*.

At the northern end of the beach is the pier, abbreviated in the Second World War by the British to stop the Germans using it in the event of an invasion. Here the Mariner's Bar, Flipper's Family Diner and an amusement arcade represent the only vestige of Nineties entertainment.

Inside the amusements, children are tugging at sleeves, asking for another 20p for the Atari Star Wars, the Sega Zoom 909, the Turbo Outrun. Those who are given only coppers make for Crompton's Double Falls, where mounds of tuppences balance annoyingly, or Derby Day, where tiny bets are placed on a plastic race you know is definitely fixed by a simple programme. If you had a couple of days here you could log the sequence and make yourself an easy £10.

But even here the influence of electro-noise is limited. The arcade is small and the parents supervise cloyingly. No wild kids fobbed off for the day with a fiver.

One of the parents is an art teacher from Leighton Buzzard, Bedfordshire, and his children are tugging at his sleeve too. He first visited Southwold in 1983, and has holidayed there for the past three years.

'But I don't think we will be coming back,' he says. 'The kids will want more excitement soon, and the place is becoming a bit trendy. The locals are very friendly but I have noticed a tiny bit of resentment this time. In the tourist office the other day the kids were told to get off a couple of chairs because they were only for people booking rooms. I've noticed a kind of Benjamin Britten atmosphere. Do you know what I mean?

'There were some hippies camping on the beach this morning and some people didn't seem to like it. I felt a bit like that too. Then I thought, Hang on, we did that in '66. It's no different really. Perhaps we're getting old.'

At the other end of town, as far as you can go, is the harbour and the River Blyth. Fishing boats and pleasure vessels are tied here at ramshackle moorage along a dirt track called Blackshore. Day-trippers dally here, their children fishing for crabs with lines and weights, using shanks of bass for bait. Couples sit in parked cars eating their sandwiches.

Southwold Sailing Club is at the western end of Blackshore. Its 215 members built the clubhouse after the war but there has been a sailing club of sorts at Southwold since at least 1850. An old flysheet on the wall advertises a regatta with a 15 guinea purse for yachts, 10 sovereigns for yawls, £3 for sailing punts, and for those without sea legs, a 20 minute duck hunt with a £1 prize.

But they don't like visitors too much.

'They are very inconsiderate,' says a member. 'They come along here in their cars, driving much too fast, whipping up the dust and that settles on your boat. First rain you get and your boat is covered in mud.'

The High Street in summer, 1997. Both cars and people throng the streets.

Single parents too, he says, bring their children along and allow them to throw stones at the vessels.

Last orders is called at the Lord Nelson, one of seven pubs on Southwold's pretty cottage-lined streets. Members of the rugby club are downing their penultimate pints. They wonder what the fuss is all about.

One says, 'All these outsiders come here and pay £100,000 for a two-up, two-down on Victoria Street. We walk up the road and over the bridge and pay £40,000 for a similar house. Why should we worry? All the money they bring here makes a good life for us, and we know it. The people moaning probably weren't born here.'

They display a spectacular talent for self-deprecating wit. 'You know there is so much inbreeding around here that even the dogs have club feet.' And of the peaceful, relatively crime-free life they lead: 'The safe was once pinched from the Crown Hotel so the police came to the rugby club to ask if we'd nicked it as a prank.'

They say there is nothing in the town to attract tourists and that's precisely what attracts them and that they are all very welcome. 'Why should we keep this place to ourselves? It belongs to everyone.' And as one of the rugby club downs the dregs of his pint he winks. 'Just keep the bastards away.'

THE INDEPENDENT
1992

Once a Village, Now a Town Corporate

THOMAS GARDNER

This place, in elder time, was called Suwald, Suwalda, Sudholda, Southwaud, and Southwood, probably from a wood growing near, for the western confines still retain the appellation of Wood's End Marshes, and Wood's End Creek.

Southwold is a sea port and town corporate in the county of Suffolk governed by two bailiffs, a recorder and other inferior officers. Distant from London, 103 miles.

Here are two annual fairs, the one held the whole three days of the Feast of Holy Trinity, the other on the Vigil, the Feast and Day following of Saint Bartholomew, and weekly, as many markets: that on Monday disused, but the market on Thursday is plentifully supplied with provisions, and other necessaries.

The Abbot of Bury had in the 5th year of K. Henry III, a grant for a market on Thursday at Southwold. And in the 11th year of that King, he had a Charter for a fair at Suwald upon the Eve and Day of St Philip and St Jacob.

The town is pleasantly situated on a hill having a descent all ways. The houses are generally well built. Here is, besides the Great Guildhall, another in the market place for the dispatch of petty affairs which with the church and other edifices afford an agreeable prospect both by sea and land.

It is bounded on the east with the German ocean, but other ways almost surrounded with the River Blith, and at high tides by both, making it an island within which the ocean on the east, and other ways with the river, a harbour wherein their whole fleet might be moored securely. And not less commodious for the encampment of their army, who could pitch their tents on dry land, from whence they might observe the approaches of an enemy from every quarter. But this is submitted.

The situation of this town being between Walberswick and Easton, places of note for the fishery, the first adventurers very likely were of the craft who for conveniency of their employment erected huts. And success attending their endeavours, more associated with them and began to build houses for habitations.

Although Southwold was a younger sister to Dunwich, Blithburgh, Walberswick and Easton, yet in process of time the inhabitants thereof not only stood in competition with those towns but surpassed them in

East Green in the early 1920s, when the greens were railed off.

navigation and traffick, growing so populous that they stood in no small repute both for trade and buildings.

AN *HISTORICAL ACCOUNT OF DUNWICH, BLITHBURGH, SOUTHWOLD*

1754

Southwold Fashioned

CHRISTOPHER MATTHEW

'Instant Nostalgia' is the phrase that sprang to the leaflet-writer's pen when attempting to capture Southwold's essential id, and who am I to attempt to top him?

But old-fashioned charm on this scale is no accident. True, Southwold is pretty isolated. Unlike most Suffolk seaside resorts, it isn't on the way to or

Gun Hill in the early 1920s showing the casino that was erected in 1810 and was used as the coastguard station until quite recently. Sam May, a famous Southwold lifeboat coxswain, is standing outside his bathing machine plot.

from anywhere. There is no passing trade to encourage those with an entrepreneurish bent to go dreaming up vulgar ways of making a fast buck and chipping away at the gentle quality of Southwold life.

Not that they would be allowed to do so. The hideous Pier Leisure Centre, with its amusement arcade and Neptune Bar – source of the cheapest beer and the only noise, such as it is, in town – was, everybody but the local biking fraternity is agreed, a sad mistake of judgement on some long-forgotten town council's part. But at least it is tucked away up at the north end of the town where few serious Southwold lovers venture, and the house prices are comparatively depressed. Any hopes that would-be developers may be harbouring, of slipping anything remotely comparable through the local planners and town bigwigs are certain to be doomed.

A year or two ago, upon learning that the harbour wall was in bad shape and that millions were going to be needed to put it right, some bright spark stepped forward to say that he would be only too happy to stand the repair bill, provided he was allowed to transform the lower reaches of the town marshes into an exciting riverside development comprising residential accommodation and (dare I whisper the word?) marina.

Many another borough would doubtless have leapt at such a generous offer, but Southwold gave him short shrift. 'WE LOVE SOUTHWOLD' declared posters in various windows throughout the town. 'SAVE IT FROM DEVELOPERS. HELP STOP THEM.'

Meanwhile, antiquated fishermen's huts are still ranged higgledy-piggledy along the shore, much as they must have been a hundred years ago – the names of the owners' boats painted above the doorways: 'Billy Boy' and 'Zulu', 'Night Out' and 'Florence May'.

Gun Hill looking south to California Sands in 1894. The *camera obscura* hut in the centre was a popular attraction: a prism in the roof reflected a panoramic view of the coastline onto a table in the darkened interior.

Whether Victorian visitors would have strolled down across the marshes to buy fresh fish from stalls like Willie's Plaice is another matter, and I doubt there would have been the black market which exists today in the rickety wooden piers, for which cruiser owners are apparently prepared to pay anything up to £3,000, plus £50 a year in ground rent.

The place is an extraordinary jumble of big Victorian and Edwardian houses, most of which have long since been divided up into flats; a few exceedingly tasty looking Regency Houses – also heavily divided – around the various greens, which came about as a result of the Great Southwold Fire of 1659; and a generous sprinkling of Victorian fishermen's cottages of various shapes and sizes.

There is also a mish-mash of inter-war, unexpectedly suburban-looking tat and council stuff – but that is mainly restricted to the area north of the lighthouse. 'South of the lighthouse' is where everybody wants to be and where the prices rocket dramatically.

The tiniest fisherman's two-up, two-down with a yard at the back in Church Street, just off the High Street, will cost you £65–70,000 nowadays; a three-bedder in Victoria Street up to £80,000; a twee picture-book cottage in or around the open expanses of the South Green will set you back a hundred at least. And only recently Adnams knocked away a three-bed terraced cottage with a garage and a little garden in nearby Park Lane for £120,000.

Even a wooden shack in Ferry Road, which runs up from the harbour past the marshes, is worth paying thirty grand for, if only for the privilege of being able to pull it down and start again, and the smallest two-bed toehold tucked away in one of the many courtyards and alleyways, which the whole place is riddled with, scores a 'most desirable' rating from the agents.

Fortunately for those keen to row themselves into this charming and expensive backwater of English seaside life, there is a surprisingly brisk turnover of property. Parents with daughters at St Felix or sons at Framlingham, who once bought a little something in order to be on hand for exeat weekends, suddenly discover that the educational caravanserai has moved on: children grow out of bucket and spade holidays and are contemptuous of notices warning that, 'It is dangerous to climb on the groynes', and yearn for more challenging distractions.

To those who can afford to stump up the sort of money it takes to step into their shoes, it will doubtless be an unfathomable mystery that anybody could bear to say goodbye to a place that can offer such multifarious delights as tutored wine evenings at the Crown, a Sailors' Reading Room, Ayckbourn and Shaw nightly at 8.15, a mayor's chair, desk and gavel made of bog oak from the ancient submerged forest of Easton Bavents, cottages with names like The Bolt-Hole and The Tittle Mouse House, and Prof. Welsh's Punch and Judy show – 'Every fine day, 11.30 and 3. On the beach below Gun Hill.'

PUNCH
1987

A Sea-Washed Town

ROBERT WAKE

The most pleasant point for enjoying as well as observing the many agreeable objects of Southwold is unquestionably the Marine Parade. Along the entire range of it are delightful walks, especially along St Edmund's Hill, the Gun Hill, and the Ladies' Walk.

Here, whether on sand or sward, the lover of nature may saunter at will. And when he feels disposed to sit there are commodiously placed benches where he can pursue his meditations as placidly as yon sweet ripple dances so lightly under the sunbeams.

How extensive and beautiful is the view which now presents itself! The splendid grandeur of the German ocean is on the one side – with its ever-heaving bosom – its hundreds of vessels moving in all directions from the slight fishing boat and single-masted skiff to the gallant gunship and

High Street looking towards the market place in 1875, showing the cobbled area in front of the Crown Hotel, shops and houses.

adventurous foreigner form a scene of admiration which is quite as untiring as it is refreshing and various.

On the other hand residence after residence presents itself – ivy-clad, or flower-fronted or tree-embowered as it may be – in fair and fantastic perspective.

Neatly latticed windows, impending balconies, picturesque garden plots, closely shaven lawns, interspersed shrubs, distant plantation clumps and gliding parties of fashionable company, afford attractions to the seaside musings at Southwold which never fail to beguile listlessness or to enchant the imagination.

What thankful and heartfelt acknowledgement of those long-continued favours and unnumbered advantages which have been providentially employed to distinguish his native land and to honour it so greatly, can the Briton experience – while he gazes upon the commanding prospect of the ever-changing deep which the overhanging cliff at Southwold spreads magnificently before him – while he sees such numerous vessels occupying their business in great waters. Some are laden with the profits and speculations of commerce, others peradventure entrusted with the nobler freightage of translated editions of the volume of Inspiration, and with self-devoted missionaries to make it known to the idol-worshipping occupiers of some yet unvisited territory.

The smooth and well-kept walks which so pleasantly intersect the sloping greens about the cliff are frequented by passing promenaders – in fashionably dressed groups, as if seemingly vying with each other as to who shall most attract the admiration so readily rendered, where all appear equally determined to be pleased.

There is a newly married couple – as their bearing towards each other may truly indicate – who are besieged by a number of young exhibitors of polished fossils, and pebbles and native agates, and cornelians tastefully arranged upon

High Street in 1926.

trays, and plates and saucers; while the unbearded aspirants after the profits of merchandise are anxious to undersell their less clamorous rivals.

In another direction, upon the sunny green where it spreads away in the distance, may be seen the cheering sports of healthful and holiday-enjoying children.

Then the undulating country beyond – fertile, rich and devious – looks no way sad by being deserted. Here and there silvery mirrors shoot out their lights upon the landscape-traversing eye, as their reflected lustre is caught by the sunbeams twinkling upon the waters of the Blythe. Indeed without designing to be partial historians in this matter, we freely declare our conviction that to the casual visitor the landward view of Southwold possesses a superiority over most other sea coast and bathing quarters in England.

One reason that we may suggest arises from the number of ornamental shrubberies and verdant and flowery parterres – and fruit-bearing trees which are so happily cultivated even among the emulous lodging houses. And still more in the handsome grounds and stately residences of the gentry which are scattered in such pleasing and acknowledged variety within the range of the cliff scenery.

The range of the Cliff, the principal point of attraction, is distinguished into three divisions each known by its respective name – South Cliff bearing the name of 'New York', Centre Cliff that of 'Long Island' and North Cliff that of 'Kill-Cock'. Centre Cliff houses present a very handsome and commanding appearance not less on account of the gracefulness of the buildings themselves, than of the loveliness with which their enclosed shrubberies and tastefully arranged and very carefully tended flower plots have contributed to their decoration.

And here we think it well to notice that the last census (1831) returns as follows for Southwold: inhabited houses, 431; number of families, 446; registered seamen, 204; total number of persons, 2,079; sum of statute acres, 680.

SOUTHWOLD AND ITS VICINITY

1839

Inns of Happiness

DAVID GIBBS

Southwold is a quiet seaside town that clings precariously to the cold, eastern edge of England. It is a pretty place with all the things a proper coastal town should have – clean safe streets, good hotels and eateries, efficient shopkeepers and law-abiding citizens.

Not much has happened in this Suffolk town in recent history. It's only real claim to fame is a fire in 1659 which destroyed most of the town in four hours.

But last year a momentous event happened. Southwold was nominated by the *Good Pub Guide*, Britain's drinking bible, as the best small pub town in England. When the news broke the local constabulary drafted in reinforcements to cope with the coachloads of tourists who arrived. I am pleased to say that good order was maintained.

Southwold's claim to fame is not unconnected with the fact that it has its own brewery, called Adnams. One of those who run it is a rosy cheeked chap called Bernard Segrave-Daly who came to Southwold originally to join the church. But the Man of Cloth became instead the Man of Ale.

Bernard certainly knows how to make an Australian feel at home. 'I do know something about Australian beers,' he said by way of greeting when I visited the town. 'I do know what they put in Australian beers – chemicals and things like that. I do know they produce a bland, cold beer that satisfies the tastebuds in a few minutes.

'But here we produce beer. It has no chemicals. It is very strong beer – you have to handle it very carefully.'

I am sure Bernard did not mean any offence. And I was assured he did not by Dudley Clarke who manages the nearby Swan Hotel, which has been Southwold's principal inn since at least the great fire.

The Sole Bay Brewery in 1872. The name 'Adnams' was first associated with the brewery in that year.

'I know that Australians are fond of their pubs,' he said. 'They will be interested to know that Southwold has the best pubs in England. That's official.'

Dudley is pretty keen on the Australian angle. 'We have tried to make overseas visitors at home here. We have a policy of employing young staff from overseas. We have even had some Australians – that has worked really well.'

There is no doubt that Dudley is a very efficient manager and the staff are indeed welcoming. That is very reassuring when staying in an English pub.

Classically English dining rooms such as that at The Swan can be off-putting to the more relaxed classes, namely Australians. But Dudley goes out of his way to foster informality. So I was bold and removed my jacket and got stuck into some local fare.

Years of living in the sub-tropics have tempered my diet and I confess to being not man enough to make it through my choice from The Swan's lovely menu.

But just in case you are made of sterner stuff this is a typical dinner: potted vegetables infused in white wine jelly with a tomato coulis; sautéed butterfly fillets of mackerel with wholegrain mustard sauce; roast leg of Welsh lamb with a redcurrant and port wine sauce; fresh raspberry and rum syllabub and sticky toffee pudding. And coffee.

Maybe it all makes sense in a cold English climate.

If English dining rooms can be intimidating, what can we say about bedrooms? A travel colleague once said that an English hotel bedroom was not a real bedroom unless the floors creaked.

Well The Swan (at least the suite that I stayed in) had wall-to-wall creaks and the horrible thought occurred to me that everyone in the hotel must know every other person's business.

But on this chilly November night, I was happy to tuck up in a rather sumptuous bed and listen to the comforting clink, clank of the old metal radiator belching out some Queensland-style warmth.

The Adnams dray delivering beer to the Crown Hotel in the High Street.

Next morning I put on a brave face and fronted the dining room again.

Notwithstanding the above I do like my breakfast. I decided I could do no wrong with the local ham and sweet pickle. I swear the ham filled my plate. I actually got a measure and found it had a circumference of 30 cm and a thickness of 4 mm.

I did the best I could, wrapped up the leftovers and it did me for both lunch and dinner that day.

After such exertions there was only one thing left to do: take a walk. Southwold has a lovely open feel. Streets dart hither and thither from the market square but it is at the end of the High Street where Southwold's past catches up with the present.

For there, overlooking a shingle beach which separates man from the grey, dank North Sea, is the Sailors' Reading Room.

Visitors are welcome to browse around the memorabilia of wrecks and lifeboats, newspaper clippings of local floods and records of regional heroes.

I say welcome guardedly. Pipe-smoking locals still gather there but how you can read anything through the fug they work up beats me.

I tried a friendly 'G'day' whereupon one member present turned to another and muttered 'Australian!'

I stayed for a few minutes before exiting, which brought forth at least a grunt.

But that's England. Charmingly self-righteous one moment, inoffensively rude the next.

BRISBANE COURIER-MAIL
1992

Discovering Southwold

ALAN BOTTOMLEY

From whichever side you view Southwold, the distant prospect pleases – whether from the northern coast road or, more usually, from that which threads the Blyth valley, from out at sea or, best of all, from across the river and marshes to the north.

Nor does closer acquaintance disappoint, nor familiarity dispel its charm. 'One of the happiest and most picturesque seaside towns in England,' writes Pevsner.

If, apart from the parish church, Southwold has few buildings of outstanding merit, there are almost none in the older parts of the town which are discordant or a visual nuisance. This is a townscape which has an infinite capacity to intrigue and draw one round the next corner through a complex pattern of small-scale streets and greens which, either in the sun or in the sea-fret, have a unique elusive magic.

Little survives of the prosperous medieval town except St Edmund's Church. Nor is there much from the following two centuries, for in 1659 a fire destroyed

Southwold from the pier in 1905, showing the row of bathing machines.

the Town Hall and market place, market house, gaol and granaries, fishhouses and malthouses, tacklehouses, brewhouses and a total of 238 buildings. Parliament declared Southwold a 'disaster area' – the first in English history.

In 1750 the port became the base for the Free British Fishery. For the next decade or two Southwold flourished and many of the grander buildings date from this second economic zenith. However, the harbour could not be kept clear of sandbanks that eventually choked both it and this promising enterprise.

At the end of the century the borough took on a new and more enduring role as a watering place; the gentry came to build or to lodge and the future was assured. Fine Regency and Victorian houses joined the Georgian. The town spread in all directions.

To the south The Common was encroached upon, gaps were filled, then in the 1890s extensive seaside suburban developments began to cover the Town Lands to the north and completed the Southwold of today.

The market place is pleasantly dominated by the splendid elevation of The Swan which has been the town's principal inn from at least the seventeenth century. Before the Restoration one landlord also acted as town clerk. It could have been money owed to the Corporation that led Robert Jacques, a later landlord at The Swan, to commit suicide in 1778.

Before 1819 the inn was a plain two storey building but then, in 1826, its owner added a third storey – note the change in brickwork. The tall pedimented bays, and probably the gorgeous iron sign-bracket which give such a festive air to the building, were added in about 1907.

The Crown was anciently called the King's Head, lavishly rebuilt about 1750 with brick 'rustications' to rival the establishment in the market place, the new Swan. It became The Crown in 1829 and perhaps it then acquired its Greek Doric portico. Good iron brackets remain, a splendid one for a lamp and another in dislocated Gothic for the sign which, with its crimped edges, has now gone. In spite of a quick succession of landlords (and landladies) and some bankruptcies, the premises were extended westwards in the mid-nineteenth century.

The King's Head is picturesque but slightly deceptive. It is in fact early seventeenth century but did not receive its first licence as an inn until 1836. Just previous to that James Maggs, the Southwold diarist, had lived there, keeping a small school on the premises. Immediately seaward it has absorbed a grocer's shop but the very handsome bowed front, Georgian and in the Doric manner, remains.

The Sole Bay Inn is four-square 'classical' with bold pilasters, cornice and brickwork in the central niche. The land on which it stands was sold in 1839 by Mary Robinson to William Tink, a Southwold bricklayer who finished his work on the adjacent site by 1841. It was probably over a quarter of a century before the Sole Bay opened its doors as an alehouse.

The visually dull Red Lion, formerly the Queen's Head, is an early seventeenth-century coaching inn, the oldest survival of the 'green before the gentry'. Insensitively rendered in cement, it has lost its shaped gables. The irrepressible bow-fronted wine shop at the corner of Pinkney's Lane dating from before 1855, when it was the shop of the philanthropic chemist Joseph Arthy, does something to redeem the situation.

At Blackshore stands the sixteenth-century Harbour Inn which has frequently changed its name – 1743, the Blackshore Alehouse; 1766, Nagg's Head; 1767, The Fishing Buss; 1801, The Ship Inn; and 1844, The Fishing Buss again, until at least 1881.

The Lord Nelson first displayed its sign not more than a decade or two after Trafalgar, and in the High Street, White Horse Cottage, possibly eighteenth century, was for a time a rather sordid beerhouse.

The brewery which dominates East Green was until recently at least benevolently unobtrusive and indeed picturesque, an entirely successful concern that is the largest employer in the borough. Adnams and Southwold are to many people almost synonymous. The benevolence is evident in the splendid lettering between its squidgy endpieces on the Old Brewery and in the painted lettering and hoist along Victoria Street.

SOUTHWOLD AND REYDON SOCIETY
1986

Local Hero

TERRY REEVE

Many Southwold residents remember vividly the awful wartime night of 15 May 1943, when German warplanes zoomed in at rooftop height without warning to attack their peaceful community, causing considerable destruction and death. They would have probably caused more if Richard Hough had not intervened.

At the time Mr Hough's squadron was called from the north to Ludham airfield in Norfolk, the Germans had been causing a lot of problems with 'tip and run' raids along the east coast.

'We decided the only way to catch the Huns was to stand by on patrol, with two aircraft at a time, 18 hours a day, flying below radar level,' recalled Mr Hough. So, despite his pleas to celebrate his coming of age in more comfortable circumstances, he spent his birthday 2,000 feet up in his Typhoon single-engine fighter in the dark in the Southwold area.

'It was about 10 p.m., at the end of our patrol, that we suddenly saw flashes in Yarmouth from guns and were warned of German aircraft coming in,' he said. They were ME 109Fs – fighters which also carried bombs – and they started dropping them on Yarmouth and Lowestoft before moving on to Southwold.

'My patrol companion, my commanding officer, lost them altogether and went home. But I had good eyesight and kept pace with them, and I saw splashes of fire from the bombs hitting this little village. At that point I couldn't do anything because I couldn't see them properly and could have done more damage to the town if I shot them down over Southwold,' he said.

So he waited for them to turn out to sea to regroup and they became perfectly visible against the lighter surface of the sea. 'I had them then. I was so angry that they should attack this little village and I pursued what I thought was the leader. I was so fast, much faster than them.

'He tried to put me off but I started hitting him with fire and hit him some more. I had about 500 rounds of 20 mm cannon and it was enough to finish him off. At the time I was firing at the one ahead, and though I didn't see him splash into the sea, it became clear I had got him too.' Most of the remaining six of the eight in the group retreated for home, but one came back on Mr Hough's tail and his plane was hit.

'Thank God I was as fast and powerful as I was and managed to outdistance him, and he went back to Schipol. But when I came back over the coast ground gunners were firing at me not knowing who I was!

'I went home shaking with excitement and later 26 machine-gun bullets and eight 20 mm shells were found to have hit my plane, which was a write-off.'

A Sunderland flying boat above South Green in 1936.

That night was the only time Mr Hough saw Southwold until he returned as a hero on Monday for the annual Trinity Fair and luncheon.

'All I could see were planes, bomb blasts and anti-aircraft flashes and it made me very angry indeed. There was no war interest in attacking Southwold – it was just a fishing village. It was good to come here for the first time this week to see it as the pleasant, peaceful place it was during those dark days of the war,' he said.

But Mr Hough remained modest about what he did for Southwold. 'It is possible that some of the German pilots saw me against the night sky and decided to go home. At the time the Typhoon was the fastest fighter in the world. And it is possible I distracted some of them and managed to avenge to some extent the death and destruction they caused,' said Mr Hough, who was mentioned in dispatches for the incident.

The raid killed 12 people and damaged 460 properties including the Town Hall, St Edmund's Church, the Congregational Church, the Methodist Church, the Roman Catholic Church, the fire station, post office, Southwold Hospital, the Marlborough Hotel, the museum, cinema and school.

It was not until eight weeks ago, through a chance remark in a London club, that anyone knew of the courageous action of Mr Hough, and his remarkable story was revealed.

He happened to ask jewellery expert Geoffrey Munn, who has a home in Southwold and who is a fellow member of the Garrick Club, where he spent his holidays. When he said it was in Southwold the ex-fighter pilot recounted his memories of that dramatic wartime night – and Mr Munn immediately took steps to let the powers that be in Southwold know.

The result was the invitation to lunch when he was thanked by the Mayor, Geraldine Bryant, by Councillor Ros McDermott in her toast to the guests and by another councillor, Brian Burrage – who lived two doors away from where one of the bombs destroyed a house – and who joked' 'I wish you had come fifteen minutes earlier.'

LOWESTOFT JOURNAL

1997

Sunny Periods in Southwold

PETER SAGER

Beloved little Southwold smells of hops and malt and sea. It lies in a dead end on the Suffolk coast, and most people – thank Heaven – pass it by. There are no sights in Southwold, no castle, no cathedral and not even any ruins. There's no reason at all to turn off the A12, cross the marsh, and head towards the white lighthouse and the bright beach huts that are lined up between fields and foam like a row of colour charts. So, please, leave the place to me.

The High Street ends in a small triangular market place in the middle of which is a Victorian pump with a glass ball and gold crown, wrought iron dolphins and the motto 'Defend Thy Ryghts'. The Swan hospitality reaches out its bay windows and gables, and opposite are the bank, Denny the Tailor, and Norman the Butcher ('over 300 years and still going strong'). It all looks as if it's always been like this, and always will be.

The first person to see us arrive is probably Ginger. He stands at his front door, blinking into the sun. Ginger wears rubber boots, one black and one green. He always wears rubber boots, in summer and in winter. People say that's where he keeps his money. Certainly he was in The Nelson once and when it was time to pay, he pulled a £50 note out of his rubber boot. His real name is Ernest Newson, but he's got this tobacco-coloured beard which is why he's known as Ginger. His father was a baker, one of seven bakers in Southwold. Today there's just one. Ginger sells lottery tickets. His pension is too small for him to be able to do any repairs on his house. If he were to sell it he'd be a rich man, for Ginger lives on South Green.

South Green is on the cliffs overlooking the sea. Only four local people still live there. The rest are 'newcomers' though some have been here for years, and some have been here before. The latter may have been here for

Ginger Newson, a local character, photographed in 1988.

their holidays when they were children and have come back again to spend their old age. Most are from London – retired judges, colonial officers, 'resting' actresses. They form a highly conservative and extremely eccentric little society. Thus, Southwold has quietly evolved into the coastal suburb of Hampstead. Half the 2,000 inhabitants are over sixty, and every sixth house is a holiday or second home. It's no coincidence that there are four estate agents here, many of the local people, especially the young, can't afford these expensive houses and so they move inland to neighbouring Reydon.

We buy our sole from Arthur Swan in Victoria Street. At fourteen 'Swanney' went to sea, at forty be became a fishmonger, and now he's nearly eighty. His bloaters, smoked over oakwood, are surpassed only by his kippers. Some customers even write poems about him: 'Whenever I am lonely / Homesick for Hertford only / I buy some fish / For a supper dish / From faithful Mr Swanney.' Even in London his fish is famous. Rumour has it that in Soho they sell his mackerel as smoked salmon.

In the middle of the town is the brewery. The sweet and heavy smell of Adnams' malt and the aroma from Mr Swan's smokehouse combine to create the heavenly scent of Southwold. There's a heavenly sound, too: at half-past eight in the morning, you can hear the hooves of the horses pulling the beer-cart along the road, and at midday they are trotting back across the market place to their stable. Prince and Sovereign have the afternoon off. Nobody overworks in Southwold.

Without Adnams, Southwold would be little more than an old people's home, especially in winter when the holiday homes are empty. Adnams' trademark is the Jack-of-the-clock that hits the bell in Southwold church with his battle-axe – a delightful link between going to church and going to the pub. Our Father followed by Our Adnams.

Towards eleven o'clock a red flag is hoisted outside the town: that means the fishermen are back, and there's fresh fish. Off we all go to the port – another of those ports that centuries of storms have driven further and further away from the town. Now it's off in the marshes where the herons breed, in the Blyth estuary. During the sixteenth century, more fishing and merchant ships went from Southwold to Iceland than from any other port on the east coast. Today there are no more than a couple of dozen fishing boats.

The harbour walls are crumbling, like bulging bulkheads. How long can they hold? Remorselessly the tide washes the mouth of the river. Bobbing boats are moored to bobbing landing-stages. Nets, planks, lobster pots, and the smell of the sea and the fish. Black-tarred fishermen's huts with blue and red doors, small ones, big ones, crooked ones, handsome ones: 'Billy Boy', 'Jackamina', 'Night Owl', 'Wyenot'.

Of course it was inevitable that one day Mrs Thatcher's investment sharks would swim ashore at Southwold. A place straight out of *Pickwick Papers*, a

South Green from Gun Hill in 1898.

Victorian Sleeping Beauty of a port. What an opportunity. They would redevelop the river and build their yachting club and sailing harbour and holiday complex. But the planners had reckoned without the people of Southwold. The only place being big enough to hold them all was the church, and the hearing turned into a tribunal. We want the huts, we don't want palaces, we love Southwold, we don't want the developers.

'We're not Brighton,' said one of the fighting ladies of Southwold, 'and we don't want to look like Bournemouth either, with flower beds all over the place and a palm tree stuck in the middle. Nor do we want to be a holiday camp for continentals. Let them go to Italy or Spain!'

After dark the beam from the lighthouse strokes the roofs of the tiny town. Don't be afraid if you should then meet the Black Man. He walks around in a ragged cloak with a blackened face like a creature from the time of the plague. His name is Robert. He has lived for many years alone on the marshes in Tinker's Barn which is knee-deep in waste paper and old tin cans. Sometimes Robert sits by the churchyard wall writing on pieces of paper from his plastic bag. Local people say he is composing. He never does harm to anyone and nobody disturbs him. . . .

EAST ANGLIA

1987

Birds of 1838

ROBERT WAKE

The natural history of Southwold itself is perhaps sufficiently distinct to be somewhat interesting.

The Common hare which before the introduction of the new game laws was abundant in the neighbouring parishes, has sometimes been found in the marshes at Southwold. And we have a tradition of one regularly swimming over the river from Reydon to enjoy the security of a seat upon The Common.

The rabbit is somewhat numerous with us, having occasionally the protection of the town council by whom a portion of the corporation land has been sometimes appropriated to the nuisance of a warren – to the exclusion of more useful occupiers. An annual rent of some £5 or £10 appears, however, to have been the temptation.

The hedgehog, common rat, blackwater rat, fieldmouse and the common mouse nearly complete the catalogue. But the polecat, in local dialect termed a 'lobster', and the weasel, in the same dialect called a 'mouse-hunt', have however been known to vex the rabbits, and it is presumed that the mole must have had its domicile in the borough as a mole-catcher was regularly retained by the old corporation whose accounts show the payment of an annual stipend of one guinea for his services.

On birds, the blackbird and the mavis have been frequently known to nest in the precincts of the parsonage, whose majestic elms some few years since afforded a cradle to the rook. This latter bird's more artificial taste in music has banished it to the wood at Reydon but it still occasionally appears among us, tempted perhaps by the larvae of the shard-borne beetle of Shakespeare, tempting also the starling which is sufficiently social to build in the roofs of our houses.

We should note our familiar friends, the redbreast and the wren, the hedge sparrow or shuffle wing, the 'muse's gayest pet' the goldfinch and that innocent and stupid bird the yellowhammer as somewhat rare among us. But the skylark, the tit lark and the linnet are numerous.

We have not been able to recognise the leader of the feathered choir, the missel thrush, as a burgess of our borough but it is usually to be heard in the opening of the year in Reydon where it annually breeds and where, although a plunderer of the cherry trees, it has protection for its song.

The kingfisher, the most splendid of European birds, is a constant resident, and by no means rare. Perhaps we ought to mention as neighbours the magpie, the feathered barometer – the green woodpecker, and its congener the middle-spotted woodpecker, which are to be seen about Reydon Wood, and that crafty plunderer, the jay.

The earliest arrival of the birds of passage is the chiffchaff. It arrives in March but retreats to the woodlands, is seldom seen and more seldom recognised and takes its departure in September. It is followed by the wheatear. Many thousands of them are taken on the South Downs in Sussex by shepherds who find ready sale for them at Brighton, Eastbourne and other towns from whence they find their way to the markets of the metropolis.

This bird was frequently recognised at Easton while Easton had its rabbit warrens and has been often shot upon our Gun Hill and common, where it has been usually confounded with the whinchat, which in April is to be seen on every furze bush.

With April comes the nightingale and its love-laboured song. It once approached so near to us as to sojourn in the shrubbery at the cottage at Reydon. In years gone by the woods and plantations of Benacre and Wrentham abounded with this bird but in an evil hour an amateur of sweet sounds with his traps and mealworms explored its favourite haunts and despoiled them of their music.

From this dark history we turn to our summer friend, the swallow. The time of its coming is in the middle of April but in the present year, although a solitary bird was seen upon the 18th, the month was altogether closed before the arrival of considerable numbers.

The swallow breeds with us throughout the summer and has usually two broods of which the last flight takes its departure early in October. The fact of its migration was, however, the subject of an extraordinary controversy – some contending it remained here during the winter, secret in hollow trees, and others that it was immersed in lakes and ponds from whence it emerged in spring.

Most modern ornithologists, however, reject this, considering it impossible.

The quail appears with us in April, taking its departure towards the close of September in which month of slaughter it has been frequently shot by our sportsmen. The landrail appears with us but rarely. It has, however, been frequently shot at Frostenden, as well as the waterrail.

The window swallow, martlet or house-martin appears with us in April, rather later than the chimney swallow, and postpones for some time any thought of preparation for a family. It builds but little in the town of Southwold, discouraged perhaps by the destruction of its nests which are more liberally tolerated in its vicinity.

The bank swallow, or sand-martin, appears about the same time but is with us in inconsiderable numbers. Some few years ago it exercised its

Dray horses grazing on the town marshes.

architectural powers somewhat appropriately in a small gravel pit within the vicinage of Skilman's from which it was driven by the levelling propensities of the pickaxe and the spade.

The swift is seen among us at the approach of May when it frequents our church in the precincts of which it may be seen to describe its endless circles and heard to proclaim an electric atmosphere with its shrilling cry peculiar to itself.

The turtle-dove is somewhat numerous near us, building in a plantation on the Wrentham road, a short distance from the bridge leading to Reydon. Its young have been sometimes taken, and a pair of them kept at the cottage at Reydon, the hen was killed by the cock bird who for some months was in the habit of pecking her head, whether out of love or mischief did not appear except in the result.

Last and the least of British birds, our visitors in spring include the golden-crested wren which is not at all uncommon in this part of the country and usually remains all the year in retreats not far remote.

The snipe has been seen with us on the 1st of September, on which day in 1825 several couples were killed in Reydon. The redwing or windthrush builds in Norway and Sweden in which countries it is said to sing delightfully and to which it commonly returns in spring. But it is presumed that some remain in this country as several young birds have for several years past been detected in pillaging the cherry trees, and shot.

The woodcock appears in larger numbers in November and after having struggled with adverse gales it has been taken by the hand in Southwold streets. It has been shot from the shrubbery upon Gun Hill, is a great frequenter of the garden at the parsonage and does not distain the shelter of the gorse upon The Common.

With the general flight of woodcocks we have the hawk owl, woodcock owl, or mouse hawk which is frequently found by our sportsmen in our turnip fields, and shot, out of ignorance, or curiosity or something worse, that is to make a bag.

The fieldfare appears in considerable flocks about the middle of October and quits in the beginning of March. Some birds remain as we have a note of a nest built in 1837 in a plantation at Reydon from which, however, some unlucky urchin took an egg or two when the nest was forsaken and the birds disappeared.

The jack snipe is generally to be met with during the winter in the rush marshes at the bottom of the Town Field where the unpractised sportsman may find daily practice with two or three of them.

The dunlin or stint appears about the same time in large flocks which tempt destruction – when shot, however, it is thrown away as worthless, although it was not so treated by our ancestors who submitted it to the culinary process and advanced it to their tables.

We should also note the ring-tailed eagle as having been shot in the grounds at Benacre with various species of hawk, whose wings may be seen stretched by captivating gamekeepers with the skins of divers vermin on various buildings.

We return to the dull record of the common seagull, the herring gull, the tern and to the heron – in the East Anglian dialect of the last century, the harnsey, which is frequently visible within our horizon, wending its morning and evening way from and to its hereditary home at Westwood Lodge.

The Blythburgh flats are a great reservoir of every species of water fowl that are known to migrate to this part of the country and we can number the curlew, redshanks, golden plover, pochard, wild duck, pintail duck, gold eye, teal and the best of the tribe, the widgeon with various others which come to us from Iceland, Lapland, the deserts of Tartary and the wilds of Siberia. Nor should we forget the wild or whistling swan, several of which were shot if not with us, near us, in the winter of 1837.

(Previous to the enclosure of the commons in Reydon the glow-worm was abundant. And was equally so at Easton before the plough had eradicated its heath. The female only is luminous.)

SOUTHWOLD AND ITS VICINITY
1839

The Royal Camp

MARGOT STRICKLAND

On 1 August 1931 the newspapers interviewed Bernard Shaw on his return from Russia. The great dramatist assured waiting reporters that black bread and cabbage agreed with him and that capitalism was doomed. On the same day 400 assorted boys, aged from 17 to 19, wearing all manner of garb from Scouts shirts to flannel bags and plus-fours, converged on London. The rendezvous was the Royal Mews, Buckingham Palace.

'Dinner will be served at 1 p.m. sharp,' they were told. 'His Royal Highness the Duke of York hopes to be present to welcome his guests.' Alas, the Duke could not be there that day but had sent a message: 'I look forward to seeing you all at Southwold.' From the Royal Mews the boys went to Liverpool Street station and boarded the train for Halesworth where they had tea, before clambering aboard a relay of buses to bring them to the quaint little resort on the Suffolk coast.

In the campsite's marquee assigned as a kitchen, chefs from Harrods, the Savoy Hotel and the Kit-Kat Club, dressed in white coats and hats, planned the menus for the week. Forty whole carcasses of lamb were to be carved up, tables were heaped with lemons to be pulped into squash, mountains of potatoes had to be peeled, and plums to be sunk into pastry for the deliciously filling plum duff, etc., etc. In the tent that served as Headquarters, the Camp Chief, Captain J.G. Paterson, and his aides planned an exhaustive programme of activities that were to occupy the boys from 7 in the morning to 10.30 at night – for one week. The camp physician Dr Archie Learoyd arranged his surgery. Sunburn was a real hazard, since boys from industrial areas rarely saw the sun. The camp chaplain assembled his texts for the morning and evening prayers. There was a resident photographer and a tuck-shop.

'Abandon rank all ye who enter here' was the motto. Bugles sounded for meals and bathing times, when 400 boys would rush across The Common, braving the thorny yellow gorse, trailing towels to the beach. It is said that one of Southwold's elderly ladies settled herself on a deckchair on the shingle, watched the boys changing and bathing and then stumped around the town complaining of their impropriety.

Accompanying the boys to the beach was the honorary Biscuit King, bearing tins of after-swim snacks, an excellent advertisement for the suppliers McVitie and Price whose principal Sir Alexander Grant was a personal friend of the Duke of York.

Nobody received a biscuit unless his hair was wet. The expression 'taking the biscuit', which has passed into the English language, derives from the camp rite when a cardboard 'certificate of merit', from which dangled a biscuit 'seal', was presented to distinguished performers at one of the nightly entertainments, 'The Order of the Biscuit'.

The most important element was the ability to mix socially. One public schoolboy who was a 'bit uppish' had a bucket of whitewash emptied over his head and he was said to have taken it 'in very good part'. A North Country lad said he was having a 'reet good time'.

On the Tuesday a heavy thunderstorm struck Southwold. Hail stones the size of golf balls fell from the sky. One of the marquees was blown over and the dining tent's central pole snapped. But by Wednesday, when the Duke of York was expected, all was shipshape again. By His Royal Highness's express desire, no civic reception awaited him.

Southwold beach and groyne.

The Dukes of York were linked with the town's history. The Battle of Sole Bay in 1672 had been fought under the leadership of James Duke of York, Lord High Admiral of the Fleet. In the twentieth century the Duke of York, later King George V, had visited the town and planted a tree. Now his son, in his turn Duke of York, was making a visit of unprecedented informality to Southwold.

The Duke was a slight figure whose nervous tension showed in his taut features. He had been a delicate youth but he had learned the value of open-air exercise: tennis, swimming and other sports had restored him to health.

After the Duke had changed, there followed a sprint across The Common, and a royal swim in the sea off the part of the beach known as 'California' opposite Ferry Road, accompanied by 400 boys. The night was spent at Eversley School which was lashed by severe mid-summer gales. The next day, as unobtrusively as he had arrived, the Duke departed.

As the Thirties progressed so did the camp. In 1933, following complaints by the boys that the straw-filled mattresses were so lumpy they fell off them and the horses they had seen in the Royal Mews were more comfortable, the pillows were filled with feathers for the first time – but the straw palliasses remained. His Royal Highness now occupied a small tent. When he was seen smoking a briar pipe the sales of briar pipes at the tuck-shop dramatically rose. A camp tie was created: stripes of red, white, green and yellow on a navy-blue silk ground.

Soon Southwold and its environs became a veritable camping Mecca. The Boys' Brigade had a camp, as did the Boy Scouts. Some 300 boys from Dr Barnardo's Homes came to camp and a party from the Bernhard Baron Jewish Settlement. Hitherto the word 'camp' had been chiefly associated with boys. But now companies of Girl Guides also arrived to pitch tents on Southwold common.

People in the town began to grumble. There were too many camps, too many boys. The caterers for the boys brought their goods with them and the local shops derived no benefit. Furthermore, the lucrative family trade that the town had depended on was being driven away by the hordes of campers. Nobody wanted to rent houses or apartments any more or book in for bed and breakfast. The press too had intruded. Photographers swarmed around the camp till a group of boys advanced on them, seized them bodily and dumped them outside the boundary rope to shrieks of 'mind my camera!'

It became increasingly difficult to retain the camp's privacy and informality. The nobility, gentry and VIPs of England descended on Southwold, from loyalty and curiosity, to see for themselves the Duke's social experiment. It had been a target for much scepticism but the idealists had emerged victorious.

When 1937 came Edward VIII abdicated and Albert, Duke of York, became King George VI. Excitement in Southwold was intense. Would the King, could the King, come to Southwold to the camp? His Majesty flew for the first time as sovereign in a twin-engined monoplane from Windsor Great Park to Martlesham, en route to Southwold, the first reigning monarch to come to the town.

By now Southwold at Bank Holiday time had come to resemble not so much a camp as an off-duty court. Etiquette was kept to the minimum and a somewhat strained spurious informality prevailed; the fiction of social equality was maintained.

The Southwold camp was to continue for one more year. In the summer of 1938 a heatwave smote the country. Boys from the factories and the mines ran about the town and The Common with startling violet and yellow legs and arms – they were being treated by the camp doctor for severe sunburn with picric and vaseline.

It was perfect weather for cruising. Escorted by a destroyer the Royal Yacht *Victoria and Albert III*, the King and Queen with the Princesses Elizabeth and Margaret Rose aboard, sailed from Spithead on their way to Scotland to anchor under a mile from the shore in Sole Bay.

The beach was crowded with thousands of sightseers waving and cheering the magnificent vessel whose figurehead of gold, red and blue spelled out the message, *honi soit qui mal y pense*.

An hour passed and 'scud' came up – a sea mist which enveloped the yacht in a cloud. Shortly before 7 p.m. a semaphore signal reached the harbour-master: 'Can you possibly send a jumping ladder up the log pier to the north of us?'

Waiting to greet the King were Sir Samuel Gurney Hoare, the Home Secretary, the Mayor Miss Florence Cohen, and the town council. At the camp a final royal repast was prepared of lamb, gooseberries and custard. Later in the day the King was rowed out to the yacht by two stalwart sons of Southwold, 'Prim' Deal, aged sixty-six, and 'Dykes' Stannard, aged sixty-eight. The yacht raised anchor and sailed on up the coast to Great Yarmouth where she weighed anchor for the night. It was a thrilling, poignant scene: a farewell from the sovereign to the little seaside town of Southwold.

This was to be the last royal camp at Southwold. Henceforward they were to take place at Balmoral. It was the end of an era. The annual excitement and disruption associated with the advent of royalty, not to mention courtiers, aides, VIPs, hundreds of camping boys and girls, families, sightseers, for one incredible week in Suffolk-by-the-sea was over. There was sadness, humility, and gratitude at the honour bestowed, but there was also relief.

The mayor in 1939, Alderman Frederick Jenkins, told the Council, 'We have lost the Camp. But there is one thing we cannot lose and that is the memory of its eight annual visits to Southwold.'

THE KING COMES TO SOUTHWOLD

1984

Southwold's Magical Christmas

JOHN MILLER

Christmas is magic and year after year in little old Southwold it has been put in its rightful place at the top of the festival tree. They come in their hundreds – thousands even – to this town perched on the pebbly edge of England to see Father Christmas, throng the square, listen to the choir and

A banner stretches across Queen Street to mark the Diamond Jubilee of
Queen Victoria in 1897.

have fun. And when the lights are turned on Southwold is a riot of colour,
and hospitality flows from shops and banks and hotels. On that Friday night
in early December Southwold is the place to be at, where it is happening.

On and off it was ever thus. Southwold has a special knack of putting on a
good show, making the most of its special character to mark special occasions.
The genesis of the business of Christmas lights almost certainly lies in the way
the town has marked the great state occasions – in this century the George V
Jubilee in 1935 and the Coronation of George VI in 1937. There were arcades
of lights, decorated floats, carnival queens, street parties and the like.

Of course the lights went out during the Second World War. But in
December 1953 they came on again to light up the lives of the people of

Southwold and Reydon and other nearby villages who had experienced the grim, dramatic events of the great flood of January that year. This Christmas Festival was really something. A handful of local traders got this particular show on the road, designing and building a wooden chalet in the market square around the pump, the very centre of Southwold life. It was a glorious structure with a man-sized Father Christmas, sleigh and two prancing reindeer riding across its roof. Around it were Christmas trees hung with coloured lights and the High Street became an avenue of fifty or more trees in Adnams' barrels.

But there was not just an opening ceremony led by the mayor, the formidable Fanny Foster, from the Town Hall balcony. There was something going on every night in the market square right up to Christmas Eve, with choirs and bands and handbell ringers and recorded Christmas music and carols, old-time dancing, and competitions – in fact, everything except a partridge in a pear tree.

Three years later these events were repeated, once again orchestrated by a handful of people who never formed a committee as such, never had a chairman or took minutes. If anything the festival was bigger and better. The centrepiece was a huge castle straight out of *Grimm's Fairy Tales*, or a Disney production. Made of timber, wire netting, hessian and plaster, with its centre cut away to form a covered stage on which performances took place for two weeks, it dominated the market square. And again every evening in the run up to Christmas the town was packed as bands played and choirs sang carols. Christmas 1965 was another huge event with two weeks of music and fun in the market square, featuring a huge Emett-style model engine driven by a Father Christmas.

The Southwold Christmas was now an established institution. One year a Nativity scene was staged on Electricity Green with a donkey as one of the star performers. But soon it was to be just one night of the year that brought young and old flocking to Southwold for what was still a magic event, if not on the grand scale of the past.

Some things have not changed over the years. There is a window-dressing competition demonstrating extraordinary flair and imagination and usually judged by a 'name'. Businesses compete enthusiastically for the best fancy dress. The Chamber of Trade plays its full part with its members opening for late-night shopping and offering hospitality. Rotary put up Christmas trees in the High Street and elsewhere and take them down when Christmas is over. Small children still flock wide-eyed to see Father Christmas at Ann Lawson's lovely grotto in The Swan yard. More often than not the weather is comparatively fine on the night. And it has remained a simple, familiar pattern.

The High Street is closed, crowds gather and shortly before 7 p.m. Father Christmas and the Snow Maiden arrive on some different form of transport (which is a closely guarded secret until the final moment). He turns up

Several thousand people flock to Southwold for the switching on of the Christmas lights, conducted from the town hall balcony by the Mayor and Father Christmas.

precisely on time, tossing sweets and waving from the top of an open bus, or a huge, slightly scary American truck, or from a coach drawn by four horses, or in vintage cars, or from a monster rocket and on innumerable, brilliantly decorated floats or trailers.

It is a mystery how the Christmas Lights Committee can come up with something different and absolutely right for the occasion night year after year. But they do. And after a brief ceremony led by Father Christmas – and he seems to get better every year! – and with a prayer and carol or two the lights are turned on and Christmas has arrived. The town is lit up and soon too are some of the folk who pack The Crown, hoping to have won one of the super prizes in the Lights raffle.

Southwold's Christmas is among the happiest in the land.

CHRISTMAS LIGHTS PROGRAMME
1997

June

LEONORA STARR

Today is Trinity Monday so this morning all acrimonious discussion concerning car parks, tennis courts, the putting green and housing was forgotten. The Town Hall was a scene of cheerful anticipation as the Mayor and councillors mustered for the opening of Trinity Fair, a ceremony that has been held in Southwold since the fair first received its charter from Henry VII, save during the two world wars.

Across the market place we made our way in the traditional procession, headed by two of the staff of the Town Hall. Junior councillors, myself among them, followed close on their heels, and last of all came a gay splash of colour where the Mayor and Deputy Mayor, aldermen, bellman and mace-bearer, in brilliant robes and old-time liveries, brought up the rear. Between the crowds lining Queen Street we headed for South Green that looked like a painting by Dame Laura Knight in the June sunlight. There we mounted the platform of the largest roundabout and turned to face our audience. Most of the watching faces belonged to holiday-makers, but the ratepayers had come thronging too, determined to extract their quota of amusement from our plight.

The bellman clanged his bell. 'God save the King!' he shouted, heralding the Town Clerk who, in his white wig, now read out the proclamation declaring that the fair was open for the 434th time.

Now came the moment joyfully anticipated by the crowds when the major and corporation must open the proceedings by having the first ride on the roundabout. 'Get on a horse quick!' someone advised me. I seized a handsome steed spotted in brown and white, only to reget it when a moment later a loudspeaker played the National Anthem. It is undignified as well as far from comfortable to try to stand to attention when one is astride a skewbald wooden horse.

Then we were off! Slowly at first, but gathering speed. The crowds broke into laughter and applause as we sped round and up and down. I scanned the faces of my fellow councillors. None showed any sign of blanching. The tempo slowed and we dismounted. Now was the moment to re-form our ranks and make our way towards the second place of proclamation, before the Crown Hotel. But no! The Mayor had other plans. Who, he cried, would follow and brave with him the terrors of the flip-flap, that some people called the octopus?

It was a challenge. Some of us in Southwold may dislike modern innovations (a certain Alderman is perpetually accusing me of wishing to live fifty years behind the times), but never yet has it been said of any councillor that he failed to carry out his duty to the Mayor. And so with bright fixed smiles we followed where he led.

The flip-flap looked more like a giant starfish than an octopus. A car to seat two people perched on the end of each long arm. I entered the first car. Somebody joined me. Suddenly we were whisked aloft and had to hang suspended high above the crowd, amid its jeers and laughter, while the others took their places.

One councillor lingered behind, ostensibly to tie a shoelace, another was delayed by an encounter with a friend, a third, suddenly absent-minded, was absorbed in watching some side-show. But all the places must be filled and so the bellman and mace-bearer were pressed into service and sat together, their clothes if not their expressions adding gaiety to the scene. The Mayor and his deputy provided another patch of colour as they smiled, side by side. I wondered whether they were feeling as happy as they looked.

The great arms started to revolve, slowly at first, then working up to a whirling speed. They sent us flying high and spinning round at the same time. Then down we swooped into the abyss, to be snatched up a moment later into dizzy skies. My companion muttered in a shaken voice that he was never a good sailor. Desperately I implored him to turn his head the other way, but he was obviously feeling far to ill to pay the slightest heed.

The Southwold and Reydon Corps of Drums lead crowds to Gun Hill for a ceremony to mark the anniversary of the end of the Second World War.

Drawing a deep breath I tried to find distraction from my own sensations in surveying the other travellers. Several looked as green as I was feeling, but Councillor Miss Foster sat at ease, not even clinging to her hat, although beside her the complexion of Dr Borham lacked its normal rosy hue, and his expression was a trifle pensive. The Mayor and Alderman Critten very creditably retained their poker faces, smiling inscrutably. I realised with faint surprise that I was smiling too, in a strange, frozen fashion. Then my world reeled again, and I held on for dear life, trying to take comfort from the fact that I was wearing my best underclothes. . . .

Our procession, heading for the second place of proclamation, seemed to lack something of its earlier precision. I noticed that our wavering ranks found difficulty in keeping step. Councillor Barber, partnering me in the crocodile, confided that he had the best thirst he had had for years.

Opposite The Crown, in the middle of the High Street, we formed a circle, waiting for the proclamation to be read the second time. Opposite I caught the eye of the alderman who often upbraids me with my supposed desire to live half a century behind the times. I wondered whether he had been converted to my point of view? There may have been no concrete bathing huts, no cafeterias along the front, no amusement parks fifty years ago. But on the other hand there certainly were no flip-flaps.

TO PLEASE MYSELF
1947

Hints to Sea-Bathers

ROBERT WAKE

Southwold appears to be increasingly benefited by numerous erections of commodious dwelling houses starting up around it. Families of respectability and fortune are gradually making it the place of their adoption and in some cases even to winter here.

Nay, some who have travelled much and are well-acquainted with the variations of our English climate and with the diversified beauties of our English scenery assert that Southwold as a winter residence is the healthiest and pleasantest of all they know.

The Bath-rooms opposite the Salt-Works should not be forgotten in a notice like this. For assuredly there must remain a refreshing recollection of them in the minds of all who have made use of their invigorating accommodation. Or by whom help has been received from the discreet and orderly couple who in a manner so quietly, kindly and satisfactorily tend their visitors. Cold, tepid, hot and shower baths can be commanded at any season in the small but convenient apartments.

The beach at Southwold also induces many strangers to sojourn among us during the summer season. Three convenient bathing machines are kept on the beach attended by strong and careful persons, affording the temptation of bathing in the sea without the possibility of observation.

These consist of a commodious wooden chamber ascended by a stepping board at one end and terminated towards the sea at the other and by an impervious curtain or awning of thick tent-like canvas, covering a kind of wooden cradle or crib floored with open boards, in which firmly secured to the framework of the machine the most timid bather may enjoy the sea without apprehension or molestation.

The cradle is terminated by the door into the sea for the ingress or egress of swimmers. This is a great improvement. For persons in sound health, and not subjected to chill from a longer stay in the water, would be little content with the boxed-in limits of a sea-water imprisonment.

The chief benefit from the bath – as indeed from all other inventions which a benign Providence has placed within the compass of man's wants and weaknesses – will be found in the judicious, well-timed and moderate use of it.

Gun Hill and cannons in the snow.

Best of all is a *single act of immersion*. This requires to be to all parts of the body at once, and made in deep water as safety and convenience may admit. Moreover the descent into the refreshing surface should be much more *gentle* than the generality of bold and ambitious bathers are wont to exercise. Meanwhile, the posture of the descending body should be much more horizontal than the rapidity and eagerness of the aquatic enterprizer will condescend to adopt.

These and other such precautions must be attended to if the sea-bather would not increase the relaxation which the bath is calculated to remove.

The time which is to be occupied is also of great importance. Bathers should know that such healthful action will not be promoted by a continuance in the bath one instant beyond the point where the thrill and glow of animal exhilaration should have begun to be experienced. And the process of drying and dressing should be dispatched as quickly as possible.

If health is to be improved by the bath, let the bath be used simply with a view to health. Conducive to this, sea bathing may indeed become – if it is used in moderation. Too frequent use of it may be as injurious to the health of the subject, as indiscreet intimacy is to friendship.

These precautions which we venture to urge upon the frequenters of our Southwold sea-quarters deserve particular attention in the case of children. To these especially, sea bathing should be so administered as to make it an object of anticipation and delight. Whereas on the contrary it is too generally a cause of alarm and dread. Such aversion has the effect of preventing the unhappy victim of it from even attempting to learn the art of swimming or of succeeding if he should attempt it.

And this is almost certain to have arisen originally from acts – nay, perhaps a single act – of injudicious and ill-managed dipping in childhood.

One plunge into the water by the hand of a gentle and encouraging attendant – with a quiet and complete immersion – will add to the courage and comfort, not less than to the complexion, of the tender but not always timid adventurer.

The loss of breath, in the case of children, when subjected to the first touch of the waves, should be as little and as brief as possible. The fright, natural to all upon first attempts of this nature, will be gradually dissipated. And the pleasurable sensation will not 'evanesce' so rapidly.

We are sincere in our impression that Southwold will present sea-bathers and fine-weather excursionists with attractions of no ordinary character. The distinctive features of this favourably situated and handsomely furnished town are: its neat and commodious lodging houses, its comfortable, capacious and well-served inns, its tastefully built and respectably tenanted dwelling houses, and its seaside and landscape scenery, graceful, complete and picturesque.

SOUTHWOLD AND ITS VICINITY

1839

Battle of Sole Bay

Naval engagements with the Dutch brought Southwold into great prominence. Most of our ancient seaports have taken a strenuous part in the battles, enterprises and expeditions that have gone to make up English history, and Southwold has borne a full share of those operations, both directly and indirectly.

The town was always ready to contribute ships, and men when they were needed for national purposes, and in comparatively modern times, that is, in the early part of the nineteenth century, Southwold was practically drained of all its male inhabitants by the press gangs, that used their own gentle methods of persuasion to recruit men to fight against Napoleon and the Yankees.

The fire beacon that once stood on the cliff was, in fact, one of the eyes of England, ever on watch for the enemy, and ever ready to blaze the signal all around the coast and country, on the first sight of the hostile French and Dutch fleets.

The fight in Sole Bay was an accident of national rather than of local history, and in fact Southwold at the time was too crippled from the effects of the great fire of 1659 to lend any decisive help in the matter. The Dutch and English navies were at the time bitter rivals for supremacy, and when they both agreed to co-operate temporarily for the suppression of the Algerian pirates, it might have been foreseen that the combination would prove a dangerous one. As a matter of fact, at every outset there was a misunderstanding and the English Government, convinced of the treachery of the Dutch, advised the king to declare war, which he did.

Accordingly, one May morning in the year 1672, the Dutch fleet appeared off the coast of Suffolk, and as the English fleet was close at hand, it almost seemed as if the sovereignty of the seas would now be decided once and finally.

The Duke of York (afterwards King James II) was in supreme command of the English fleet with the Earl of Sandwich, Admiral of the Blue, and Prince

Rupert, Admiral of the White, and he had made Southwold his headquarters. He took up his residence at Sutherland House, which has now become the home of an excellent boarding school for young ladies, with the French and English fleets anchored in uneasy alliance along a line between Easton Bavents and Minsmere. The Dutch did not delay. In fact they appeared so suddenly that the English cruisers, acting as scouts, only barely saved the English fleet from being completely surprised.

As it was, many of the ships had to hastily cut their cables, and a considerable number of officers and men who were carousing in the Southwold hostelries found themselves quite unable to rejoin their vessels and had to look on at the engagement as helpless spectators on terra firma.

They were not the only excited spectators. Crowds of farmers and others rushed into Southwold from outlying districts and the local authorities, for the defence of the town in case the Dutch might overcome the English, placed a strong guard on the bridge to prevent the incomers from leaving the town until all the danger of an invasion was over.

But it never came to that. The battle went on all day until the Dutch vessels, being badly shattered, were obliged to retreat, and the English having suffered in an equal degree were in no condition to pursue them. The Dutch, led by the famous De Ruyter, lost only three ships but their loss of men was supposed to have been very great. Considering the disparity of force after the defection of the French – generally believed to have been done on secret orders, in the expectation that the Dutch and the English would wipe each other out – it cannot appear surprising that our fleet should have suffered still more severely. Two English ships were burned, three sunk and one taken, and about 2,000 men were killed and wounded. The Earl of Sandwich went down with his ship and his corpse washed up some days later could only be identified by the star he wore on his charred uniform. The English fleet claimed victory. But it was of a doubtful nature.

SOUTHWOLD AND NEIGHBOURHOOD

1900

The War Years, 1938–45

J.S. HURST

In the early autumn of 1938, when trouble seemed to be brewing and it was touch and go whether there was to be war, the local Territorials were mobilized during the crisis and departed on war duty. And in anticipation of the worst occurring, trenches were dug in various parts of the town to give shelter in case of air raids. The crisis past, the Territorials came home and the temporary shelters were filled in.

International affairs, although quietened down, were in a critical condition and the government, to be ready for any emergency, began the Air Raids Precautions Scheme, and recruitment and training commenced. Air raid wardens, Red Cross and ambulance parties, road repair gangs, decontam-ination, rescue services, a reorganized fire brigade and the Special Police all started training in their respective duties. Equipment was procured, gas masks supplied to all inhabitants and 15 concrete air raid shelters were constructed, sufficient to hold 450 people. First aid posts, hospitals and rest centres were also arranged.

And then in September 1939 the blow fell. But as far as civilians were concerned Southwold was ready.

The early part of the war was very quiet. The Grand Hotel, Centre Cliff schools and numbers of empty premises were requisitioned by the War Office for the use of the soldiers. Recruits came and went and did their preliminary training while experienced soldiers sandbagged and barbed-wired and erected defence points.

The Government, considering London to be the main target of the enemy aircraft, carried out a huge evacuation scheme of women and children and a large number were sent to Southwold. They were brought to Lowestoft by boat and from Lowestoft to Southwold by buses. They were then sorted out and billeted with local householders.

The children stayed here quite a time, but then came the evacuation of Dunkirk, and the prospect changed, and instead of affording shelter for evacuees our own people became evacuees – mothers and their children and elderly people were ordered to leave.

This reduced the population to less than 800 people, just under a third of the normal population.

Military engineers and contractors erected defence works practically all round the town – tank traps, obstructions, minefields, steel scaffolding, sparked girders concreted into the beach, and all the devices they could think of to delay and keep an enemy at bay.

Naval guns were placed on the Gun Hill and near the harbour – one morning shoppers were surprised to see a big lorry carrying bales of hay up the High Street, until it was seen the hay all but covered the mouth of an enormous gun. The railway bridge was blown up. A hole was blown in the pier. A boom was put at the mouth of the harbour and two boats were sunk in the fairway.

Southwold was now to all intents and purposes a garrison town, full of troops. In addition to the Civil Defence services the Home Guard was formed, and went through intensive training.

Southwold looked a sorry place now. More houses appeared to be unoccupied than were in use. No visitors were allowed to come as it was a prohibited area. Life was exciting to everyone who was left, and if capable each was given some duty. The streets had to be patrolled each night by fire-watching patrols, and a large number of women joined in this work.

There were some exciting and dreadful events. A minesweeper was sunk a short distance from the pier. Three German planes were seen to attack a patrol boat. Bombs dropped all around it, but without a hit. A 5,000 ton ship came ashore, damaged and afire at South Cove; the crew was rescued

A winter scene in 1995

and brought to Southwold. A nasty shock happened one afternoon when the minefield on the beach from the lifeboat house to the harbour went up. About sixty mines exploded almost simultaneously.

It was in 1943 that Southwold was worst hit. In February a lone German bomber dived out of the clouds and without warning dropped one 1,000 lb high-explosive bomb at the rear of the houses on the south side of Pier Avenue, near the pier. This made a crater 60 ft by 30 ft deep and demolished one house, partly demolished seven others and damaged a further twelve. Luckily no one was killed; the only serious casualty was Mrs Rita Field, who had one eye damaged.

On a Saturday night in May seven German bombers approached, flying low over the sea towards Lowestoft, then appeared to have spotted barrage balloons over the port. So the planes turned inland, and then out again over Southwold dropping four bombs from a low altitude. One bomb hit The

Common and bounced through the roof of Wymering House, in the High Street, and landed on Bartholomew Green in front of the church, demolishing a house and trapping the occupant.

All the church windows were blown in and the church itself was smothered with broken glass, brick rubble and dust. Surprisingly very little structural damage was done, sandbags saving the lower part of the famous rood-screen. By Friday the church had been cleaned sufficiently to hold the funeral services of the seven people killed.

There were few other incidents after this raid until February 1944 when over 1,000 incendiary bombs fell across The Common. A large number fell on the town in March, damaging some houses.

In October German flying bombs, called Doodle Bugs, began to cross the coast. Several of them fell in the neighbourhood or were shot down. One passing over Southwold was hit by anti-aircraft guns on The Common, and the blast caused damage to 616 buildings. This appears to have been the last incident in Southwold.

The town's wounds were many. The front was badly damaged, beach huts – most of which were placed about on The Common to act as obstacles to landing by enemy planes – and all amenities went. The Grand Hotel was put out of commission. Two hotels, the Marlborough and the Dunwich, were demolished by bombing, together with nearly all the houses in Marlborough Road. All the bungalows on Ferry Road were either demolished or badly damaged. St Edmund's Hall and the Constitutional Hall Club were also destroyed. The whole town looked shabby and in disrepair, with house and shop windows boarded up through lack of glass.

In all seventy-seven buildings were destroyed by enemy action, and in the bombing raids thirteen Southwold people lost their lives. There were 2,046 warnings of the approach of enemy aircraft, and 119 bombs and 2,689 incendiaries were dropped.

STORY OF SOUTHWOLD

1956

Southwold as a Health Resort

Having set forth a few of the claims of Southwold to be considered as distinctly one of the most interesting and pleasant watering places on the Suffolk seaboard, we would now add a few words relative to its almost unrivalled advantages as a health resort. Skilled physicians may do much to mitigate the troubles of the confirmed valetudinarian, or to assist the convalescent in regaining nerve and vigour but there is also such a thing as *vis medicatrix naturae* – the healing power of nature – and where we may ask can there be found a purer atmosphere or more healthful breezes than in Southwold?

Southwold is now pretty generally acknowledged to be probably unrivalled as a health resort among English watering places. It has hitherto

August bank holiday, 1905. A huge crowd is watching the annual lifeboat launching and display.

been too much in the vogue to assume that a bracing air is unsuitable to invalids, and unfortunate sufferers have for years been sent in thousands to watering places that are notable chiefly for their mild relaxing climate.

Many of those resorts along the South Coast are exposed to the dangerous fogs exhaling from the Channel owing to the influence of the Gulf Stream, and a residence to such places often proves so unervating as to entirely prevent permanent recovery, by unfitting the invalid of living elsewhere.

The pure, bracing, clear sea air of Southwold, on the contrary, builds up, strengthens and consolidates. The sea air, travelling over thousands of miles of ocean before reaching the east coast of England, arrives here charged with ozone, and is unrivalled for its purity and bracing tonic influence and this explains to a large extent the marvellous benefits which invalids and young persons derive from even a short residence at Southwold.

If any authority be needed as to the peculiar virtues of Southwold sea air we have but to refer to Sir William Gowers MD FFS, who says that Southwold possesses characteristics that qualify it to be called one of the most bracing resorts to be found. Its restorative power for all forms of general and nervous debility are remarkable and from May to October sufferers from phthisis [consumption] derive great benefit and if further evidence is required of its restorative properties we have but to quote from a useful and interesting book on the climatology of Southwold by the Medical Officer of Health, Dr A. Corbyn Herbert. He says 'Chronic invalids as well as convalescents quickly show signs of returning power. The bracing air seems to give them new life and spirits and energy to rise superior to their afflictions and to shake off the dullness of despair that has come upon them.'

Such testimony as this of the healing properties of the air of Southwold is indisputable.

The town is well supplied with medical comforts of every description and the bright, cheerful surroundings of the place combined with quiet and restful seclusion count for much in the restoration of health, not only in the case of actual invalids, but also in the case of those whose mental and

The Adnams dray returning to the town from the Harbour Inn.

physical powers have become temporarily exhausted from overwork or anxiety. Indeed it seems almost as if those who most keenly enjoy the charms of Southwold are those whose physical or mental sufferings need solace, for previous suffering adds a zest to the present joy and, 'If misfortunes ne'er clouded the light of our day, Our pleasures would half of them wither away.'

The death rate is exceedingly low, only 11 per 1,000, and in 1896 it was only 7.5 per 1,000, and Dr Herbert says: 'The longevity of life in Southwold is one of its characteristics. Many old people of 80 years of age and upwards are still at work and I have now before me a list of 30 persons all over 80 (three of them over 90) who are going about in the enjoyment of very fair health and there are probably more. Half the total number of deaths is usually made up of those over 65 years of age.'

SOUTHWOLD AND NEIGHBOURHOOD
1900

From Now On, Home Is Where The Hut Is

ROHAN DAFT

Beach homes can cost less, much less, than the one million dollars John Cleese and his American wife Alyce Faye have paid for their three bedroom, glass-walled beach retreat in Santa Barbara, 100 miles north of Los Angeles.

Mine cost £8. Admittedly, a modest affair, perhaps resembling a dignified garden shed with wooden walls and just one room; but to me it was home with a view to rival none other in Los Angeles or anywhere else for that matter.

£8 was the hire fee I paid for the use of a beach hut at Southwold, Suffolk. Most people have the impression that beach huts are available and used solely

The promenade at North Cliff in 1980.

in the summer months. But that is not the case – I hired my hut, or chalet as some would prefer it, for the weekend. And a brisk, bright October is the finest time to visit the Suffolk coastline.

Southwold is often acclaimed as our *nicest* seaside town. Life there is, outwardly at least, gentle: an air of Victorian primness permeates. But it is also the sort of place that you could imagine the *News of the World* getting to grips with. It is a popular retreat attracting artists and writers, or bohemians as the local guides prefer to call them and, for a provincial town, there is a remarkable whiff of both money and gossip in the air.

The shops and the tea rooms might appear a shade touristy, but they remain the right side of twee. The main street is the High Street where you'll find two excellent hotels.

There are a couple of hundred huts placed with sentry-box precision along the front. Most of them are painted, many of them green and blue and some, my favourites, Battenburg–cake pink and yellow. And the vast majority of them have names. Mine, alas, was not painted – resembling as it did a creosoted garden shed with a balcony – but it had that certain charm that they all possess. It was called 'Poles Place', which, while not a bad name, didn't quite grab me as much as 'Camila' 'Nautilus' or indeed 'Valium'.

The interior of the hut measured 7 feet by 6 feet, and against one wall there was a Formica-topped table upon which stood a single-ring gas burner, a corkscrew, a blue and white coffee pot, a milk jug and six mugs. There were also two folding upright chairs, and six of those ghastly white plastic stacking chairs that have managed to infiltrate even the chic Parisian Tuileries. How I longed for a stripey deckchair. In the corner there was a small and delightfully English curtained-off area to get changed behind. I spent most of Saturday, as generations of English have before, walking along the front or sitting well wrapped up on my balcony reading, soothed by waves and the autumn sun. More of the same followed on Sunday morning before a thirty minute stroll over the dunes and through the harbour for a lunchtime drink in the neighbouring village of Walberswick.

Children sat on the estuary wall with their string and bacon, hauling up crabs: an innocent pleasure. On the way back I bought a crab and some smoked haddock in the harbour to take home. I suppose, had I not already decided on lunch, I could have cooked them on the gas burner in my hut.

There aren't many things you can't do in a beach hut – except sleep.

EVENING STANDARD
1994

Shrimps and Golf

RICHARD SISLEY

The sole, the herring and the shrimp were undoubtedly the oldest inhabitants of Sole Bay. And they attracted the first human settlers to Southwold. As early as the time of Edward the Confessor the place was famed for its herrings; and in the Domesday Book they are mentioned as the chief product of the place.

Fishing has always been the mainstay of Southwold and the fisher folk live on from generation to generation with little change in their habits: generally marrying among themselves, fishing in the season and watching the sea from the leeside of a shed in stormy weather.

Of late years fish has been less plentiful. And at Sole as elsewhere the steam trawler is execrated by the people. Yet the visitor to Southwold will be unfortunate indeed if he does not get fish. Let him rise early and catch the boats as they come in. He will have no need to quarrel about the price and he will be unlucky if he does not in the same pilgrimage get both an appetite and a breakfast.

The shrimp is superior to that of Pegwell Bay. He is large, brown and succulent and he should be eaten as soon as he has been boiled. A distinguished physician of my acquaintance has ordered that, in the case of his hospital patients, the carapace and horny external coverings should be removed before eating. He added that should difficulty arise, the hard part should be carefully extruded from the mouth. But let the visitor to Sole dismiss from his mind the recollection of all former shrimps and approach the dainty without preconceived objections and try the Southwold shrimp *au naturel*.

The sea has encroached considerably since the Norman Conquest but the town has suffered less from its inroads than Dunwich or Easton, its next neighbours on the north and south. These sudden inroads or swipes are produced by strong winds. A few years ago one of the oldest Southwold families lost several outhouses in a night which were all washed away in a few hours.

The most observant of sailors will not prophesy the direction of the next swipe, nor the time of its advent. But there is a fair agreement among them that a threatened promenade pier would be likely to have an ill effect on the foreshore. Up to the present Southwold has been mercifully spared from such an infliction. Nor have peripatetic singers received sufficient encouragement to remain. The town band, which is not so bad as it might be, plays only at rare intervals. A few years ago a rather attractive Salvation Army lieutenant came, and her likeness appeared in the photographer's window. The ground, however, proved stony and the Army has evacuated, possibly for strategic purposes.

It must be supposed that the place is free from all nuisances. There is the 'summer man' as he is called, with loud check knickerbockers and an affection for golf. There is also the female golf-pirate. There are invasions by steamer, and rail, and by coach from Lowestoft and from Yarmouth and Cromer. If you are staying at the inn and you take lunch, hasten on first sight of the steamer, and eat. These Lowestofters are as locusts. Yet why complain? Are there not nine months (Bank Holiday times always excepted) when there are no summer men and no pirates?

The golf links are out on The Common: a fine breezy place from which there are splendid views of the sea and Dunwich Bight, of the ruins of Walberswick church, and inland of the valley of the Blyth. But these names, to those who know them not, are but as the crackling of sticks upon the fire. And only in those who have seen the sun set behind the tower of Blythburgh, and the mists rise in the valley of the Blyth will they, perchance, recall a vision of the past.

A golfer naturally cares more for the hazards than for the distant view; and his vision is not beyond the next hole. Let me therefore confess at once to the professed golfer that there are only nine holes. On the other hand there is no cross-firing and the expert may exhibit his skill as much by a judicious 'loft' across 'the pit' as by making a long drive towards Skilmans.

The Common fortunately is not entirely monopolized by golf. There is room also for cricket and for lawn tennis (such as it is). I have never heard that any visitor has yet been disabled by a stray golf ball. I mention this because 'in another place' two ladies were lately hit within a short space of five minutes and one of them was told, by way of apology or of explanation, that golf links were dangerous places for ladies.

Southwold golfers do not forget that The Common is not their own private property and it is to be hoped that visiters will not consider it is entirely theirs. Unfortunately, The Commoners have allowed some houses to be built upon their property, and have quite recently granted to a waterworks company a site on which a most hideous building has been erected.

However it may be hoped that no further encroachments will be allowed and that the generous offer by the Corporation to grant ground for a golf house will be the last concession made of the commoner's rights.

Let them rigidly prevent any further absorption of their property into private gardens. Not that there are not members of the Corporation who look after their rights, and who are on the alert. It is not so many years ago that the present secretary of the golf club first marked out a tennis court on The Common. To him came a town councillor, inquiring what he was about. He feared the chalk marks were the proposed site of a house.

With the exception of the beach Southwold does not appeal to the artist but from the bathing machines under the north cliff to those on the south beach the shore is full of interest. At Southwold the unusual custom prevails of not separating the bathing places and so it is a common thing to see a husband and wife, or father and mother and growing up boys and girls enjoying together their morning swim. Under the cliff all along the shore are net houses where the fishermen keep their tackle, and beached on the shingly shore are about a hundred fishing boats. Somehow one associates with a fishing beach bad odours and messes generally: it is not so at Southwold, and yet the picturesque is everywhere, from the fisher children playing on the foreshore to the men themselves mending their nets or sorting their fish.

PALL MALL MAGAZINE

1893

Into Eden, East of Ipswich

BYRON ROGERS

The great thing about Heaven, said St Thomas Aquinas, was that it allowed those who got there to look down on those who had not. If you want to anticipate the experience have dinner one night in The Crown at Southwold where England and the North Sea are at each other's throats. But do *not* eat in the dining room, where tables may be reserved (the claim that you could book tables in Heaven prompted the backwash which became known as the Reformation); you must eat in the bar, where they may not.

The food is superb. The menu changes every day but this is a typical march past: whole local plaice grilled with lemon, lime and capers; baked fillet of huss with green peppers and wholegrain mustard; roast beef and Yorkshire pudding; casserole of Suffolk pork. And so it goes on with whole Dover sole, steamed skate, hut clafoutis (whatever that is) of roasted vegetables. There are no bar snacks like these anywhere in England, and at The Crown you are free of the tyranny of three, four and five course menus.

The wine list is as elegantly bound as a medieval missal, but it is not that which is remarkable so much as the fact that twenty wines can be bought by the glass. Still, you might not choose to drink wine at all for where you are is a place as legendary to beer drinkers as the Blue Rock Candy Mountain. Adnams Brewery is in Southwold, so if you drink in either of their two show-piece hotels, you drink at the Brewery Tap.

The result is that when The Crown opens at 6.30 p.m., within fifteen minutes every chair and every table is occupied, for to order dinner you need a table but you still may not order until 7.00 p.m., when the handwritten menus, like exam questions, are produced. 'To order earlier would not be fair on the other diners,' a barman solemnly told me. So those who come late cannot eat at The Crown.

The old hands among them admit defeat, peering in and then departing into the night. But others make for the small bar and stand there in the hope that their presence, supperless and shifting from one agonized foot to the other, will shame diners into bolting their food and vacating their tables. It is the most extraordinary social situation.

The latecomers look around them piteously, trying to catch someone's eye, but the diners eat stonily on, some in sheer bloody-mindedness rampaging through the puddings (chilled lemon parfait, hot fresh fruit crumble with custard), even establishing a beachhead among the dessert muscat wines.

Believe me if you want to see man's inhumanity to man come to The Crown at Southwold during the school holidays when whole families come, many being called but few chosen. Come for the drama – not of the dinner, which is excellent, but for the diners.

For in the end the standing latecomers despair, and then, scattering reproachful looks on all sides, they hand in hand with wandering steps and slow, through The Crown bar, take their solitary way. Milton who so described Adam and Eve being flung out of Eden must have eaten at The Crown or somewhere very like it.

Please don't think I am overdramatizing this – it is what happens every night, and is worth the long trek through the marshes.

SUNDAY TELEGRAPH
1995

Pride of the Ages

ARTHUR MEE

Half of it lies in the sea and no man can say when the waves will swallow up the other half of old Southwold. Yet it has been a prosperous place since the days of Edward the Confessor when its fishermen paid 20,000 herrings every year to the lord of the manor. We have seen complaints that it is one of the few fine towns without a station, but it has much to see and one noble possession it has, beating all the railway stations in the land, is a medieval church which sweeps in beauty from end to end. In all our ten thousand visitings we remember no country church more beautiful than this, a stately village cathedral, impressive and full of colour, reminding us of the glory of our churches in their great medieval days.

A forlorn-looking place when our century opened, the church has been lovingly restored so that we see it much as it was when the rich wool merchants built it. A veritable delight to look upon, it is one of the most perfect barn churches in the land, its nave and chancel and aisles enclosed in walls without a break, its windows magnificent, its medieval tower rising 100 feet with chequer-work of coloured flints and stone, giving it a beauty not to be forgotten. Above it swings a fisherman's boat as a weather vane. An inscription in stone with a crown over each letter begs St Edmund to pray for us, and on the arch of the tower door below is a dragon and a leopard. All round the church is a fine array of heads.

St Edmund's Church, with small admirer, in about 1900.

The white wolf of Henry VII, who gave Southwold its charter, is on the archway of the two storeyed porch, a place magnificent, with a grand old door carved on both sides. It has richly panelled battlements and a canopied niche between its upper windows, and in the roof are badges and bunches of fruit, while in a panel is a crowded head and the figure of a cock below the arrows of St Edmund's martrydom.

In the upper room (with a secret latch) is a small museum with the stocks and whipping post (of which copies are on the little green outside) and a fourteenth-century chest. Inside and outside of this church are about a hundred mason marks, some of them finely cut initials and some curiously like insects.

The splendid porch brings us into a splendour greater still, a church 144 feet long and 56 feet wide, with the peak of a glorious roof 66 feet above the floor. 'What a place to sack' the fanatic Dowsing must have said as he came in with his hatchets and hammers to smash these windows, to break up these saints and angels, and to wreck what he could of the woodwork. Splendid it all is in spite of him: the great east window, with 50 figures of

Southwold clergy on Southwold beach in 1988.

glass, has 20 tons of stone in its framework. The nave roof is a masterpiece, with its wooden angels jutting out from the hammerbeams.

The church is rich beyond most churches in its screens, for it has three from the fifteenth century. The wonderful chancel screen runs across the church, one of the richest and daintiest pieces of medieval woodwork in Suffolk. It has thirty-six painted panels which have been restored so that we may see them as their fifteenth-century artists left them: one has a picture of the old church before this.

The stalls of the chancel are carved with a richness reminding us of those in Henry VII's Chapel in Westminster Abbey. On the arm-rests are angels, grotesques and animals and on one stall is a carving of the mouth of Hell.

The medieval pulpit draws all eyes to it with its vivid colour. It is one of the finest pulpits in the country, its tracery outlined in gold with flowers and other rich ornament, all splendidly restored in our time by the daughter town of Southold, Long Island, in America.

The carving on the huge walnut chest, a splendid figure of St George full of energy, was done more than 500 years ago. The chest itself is one of the best in England.

The altar table (with a lovely embroidered modern cloth) is Elizabethan, and above it are five panels painted by a modern artist.

All through the long life of this great church has stood here a young soldier called Jack the Smiter. He has kinsmen at Dennington, Wells, Wimbourne and other places and his duty is, like their's, to strike an hour bell with sword or battleaxe. Southwold Jack is about 4 feet high, carved in wood, and wears armour of about 1470. His head is made to turn by the same mechanism that raises his arm to strike the bell. A queer helmeted fellow, he is one of the most popular figures in Suffolk.

Preserved in the church is a stone with a reference to two wives, and in the churchyard is the grave of two sisters. The wives were those of Thomas Gardner, a customs officer who wrote a history of Dunwich, Walberswick and Southwold, and the stone refers to his book and his wives: 'Betwixt Honour and Virtue here doth lie, The remains of Old Antiquity'.

The two sisters are Agnes Strickland and her biographer Jane. Agnes, the best known of the nine children of the Strickland family, is famous, with her sister Elizabeth, for the work they wrote together, the *Lives of the Queens of England*, which has been steadily read for nearly a hundred years.

THE KING'S ENGLAND
SUFFOLK 1941

The Southwold Railway

J.D. MANN

The crumbling coastline of East Suffolk remains remarkably unspoilt and the elegant old borough of Southwold, in its Edwardian heyday, began promoting its genteel atmosphere and attracting discriminating holiday-makers with the promise of 'private bathing' and a dry, sunny (if a little breezy at times) climate.

It no doubt came as a bitter disappointment to the town when the East Suffolk Railway decided on a more inland route – some nine miles away at Halesworth – for its line from Ipswich to Yarmouth. Applications for a branch to Southwold fell on stony ground. The idea for a lower coast narrow gauge line evolved from a meeting with several railway engineers including Mr R. Rapier of Ransome-Rapier, Ipswich, who had gained experience of such railways and equipment, having already designed locomotives and rolling stock for the ill-fated Woosung Tramway of China.

The decision having been made, the 3 ft gauge Southwold Railway opened for business under its own Act of Parliament on 24 September 1879.

From its own station at Halesworth the unusual little train passed over the Holton Road on a girder bridge, then turned coastward past the engine shed and water-meadows to the first station at Wenhaston. The train continued close to the River Blyth and then took a wide sweep around the magnificent church before coming to a halt at Blythburgh station.

The following was undoubtedly the most delightful section, through the heronry with views over the wide estuary mud flats and on to Walberswick station set on The Common among the gorse bushes. The final part of the journey took passengers over Tinkers Marsh and the swing-bridge over the Blyth to Southwold station near the entrance to the town.

The Southwold locomotives were rather attractive with tall chimneys and carried names as follows: no. 1 'Southwold', no. 2 'Halesworth' and no. 3 'Blyth'. With the expansion of services planned, especially on the harbour branch at Southwold, a further locomotive, no. 4 'Wenhaston' – a far more substantial engine and differently designed to the others – was delivered in 1914.

Ironically it was no. 4, having handled much of the traffic in the final years, which was entrusted to work the last train in 1929, the railway having

Southwold railway station in its heyday. The line, which ran nine miles to
Halesworth, closed in 1929 after fifty years' service.

suffered from increasing road transport plus a curtailment of fish traffic due
to the outbreak of the First World War.

The last passenger train from Southwold was the 5.23 p.m. on Thursday
11 April and was a carnival affair. Despite the bitterly cold weather, several
hundred people gathered in the station premises to give the well packed train
– there were 150 aboard – a rousing send-off. A wreath of laurels was placed
on the coupling hook of the locomotive, which was in the charge of the
brothers Stannard, and after the stationmaster's bell gave official sanction for
the journey to commence, the train drew slowly out of the station with two
extra coaches to deal with the anticipated crowd for the return trip. One
passenger at least, Major E.O. Debney, had travelled on the first train nearly
fifty years before. On its return there was a prolonged whistle as the engine
entered the cutting on Southwold common. Crowds sang 'Auld Lang Syne'
as the train drew in. As the coaches were shunted to the bay for the last time

and the engine taken to the shed, three loud cheers went up and the proceedings were over.

After closure the railway soon began to steadily decay, various schemes to reopen the line fell by the wayside, and nature reclaimed the track and stations. By 1940 the decline had become so great that a revival would have been almost impossible. By now the Second World War had begun and the Ministry of Supply, desperate for scrap metal, put out directives for the recovery of suitable materials from little used railways.

The Southwold branch fitted very nicely into this category and demolition began in 1941. By early 1942 the little line was no more. Today only odd pieces of track come to light occasionally and a short length complete with sleepers can still be seen at low tide on an old harbour branch at Blackshore, having survived the ravages of the sea for over sixty years.

SUFFOLK LIFE
1996

The Grand Hotel

It has been gravely asserted that the average Englishman 'takes his pleasures sadly' but who would endorse the libel when travelling swiftly and smoothly on the bosom of old Father Thames and thence down the North Channel on one of the splendid saloon steamers of the Coast Development Company? There is something soothing and restful even in the thought that one is leaving the smoke, din and bustle of the vast Metropolis for purer air, more invigorating surroundings and the comforts and luxuries of an exceptionally well-managed hotel.

We are supposing of course that the voyageur is bound for sunny Southwold in general and the beautiful Grand Hotel in particular – so he had a real good time before him and will certainly depart with a proportionate amount of regret.

One of the greatest charms of this splendid hotel lies in the fact that the intending visitors can travel by the fine Belle saloon steamers direct from London Bridge almost to the very doors of the Grand itself, the sea trip being in itself an ideal holiday. In fact one gentleman whom we have frequently met, and whom we hope to see again – a retired officer and one who held a high position under Government – has assured us that the trips he takes on these steamers twice or thrice weekly are absolute life to him, and build him up and fortify him for the winter.

The panoramic views of the shipping, wharves, docks and factories as the boat ploughs through the water at the rate of about 20 miles an hour, are not likely to be easily forgotten. Quickly we glide past Greenwich with its world-famous naval hospital, then Woolwich, its Arsenal and dockyard, the storehouses of vast quantities of warlike material, on by the quaint old-world town of Gravesend on the one hand and Tilbury Docks and fort on

The beach and pier in 1908. The pier was built in 1900 and was a stop for the Belle steamers that ran between London and Great Yarmouth.

A crowded South Green in 1997, at the time of the Bugatti car rally.

the other, on, still lower down the stream past training ships, floating hospitals, and gunpowder magazines, to giddy Southend with its mile and a quarter of pier, and then getting right away to sea we steer direct for frivolous young Clacton and onwards to that other 'blushing bride of the sea', Walton-on-the-Naze. Harwich and the rivers Stour and Orwell are passed in quick succession and then we speed forward past fashionable Felixstowe and so on past Bawdsey Ferry to Alderton, Orford Castle and the Ness until Aldeburgh and Dunwich being left behind we are landed on the quaint little pier at Southwold.

Almost regretfully we hand ourselves and our baggage over to the obliging porter and shortly afterwards find ourselves comfortably ensconced within the hospitable portals of the Grand, ready to do ample justice to the daintily served dinner awaiting our sea-sharpened appetite, a fitting termination to a most healthful and enjoyable day.

The Grand Hotel is in every sense of the term an ideal resting place. It has been recently erected from the designs of C.H.M. Mileham Esq. and is fitted throughout in the most perfect manner. The drawing room is a picture, its decorations being in the most artistic style and in keeping with the Chippendale and other high-class appointments which have, as well as the furniture of the other rooms, been supplied by Messrs Shoolbred. A very handsome dining room to seat about 100 visitors faces the sea and is brilliantly lighted by electricity. The billiard room is in every respect worthy of the house and has a fine antique inglenook.

There is a pleasant recreation room for children, a reading room, smoking room, a handsome lounge and some 100 comfortable bedrooms, most of them facing the sea. The hotel is heated throughout the winter by radiators and there is an Otis Safety Elevator to all floors. A strong room for the deposit of valuables is a useful adjunct and in fact there seemed to be nothing wanting to minister to the complete comfort and convenience of visitors. Needless to say the sanitary arrangements have received especial attention and are as perfect as modern science can make them.

Surrounding the hotel are well-kept private gardens and tennis courts while there are good golf links near by which are open to visitors, providing a fair abundance of those characteristic difficulties which the fervent golfer lives to overcome. The Grand too is a regular rendezvous for gentlemen who frequent Southwold during the shooting season for wild duck, snipe, widgeon, teal, wild geese, etc. Boating and fishing are also much patronised by visitors, the boatmen being steady and experienced obliging men whose charges are very moderate.

And now in conclusion let us just add a word or two in reference to the general management of this elegant and luxurious hotel. Both the manager and manageress are courteous and obliging to a degree. The service is excellent – every want and requirement of visitors being forestalled in a wonderful manner. Of the cuisine we can pass very high encomiums indeed while the charges are throughout as moderate as is consistent with high-class catering and visitors can be received *en pension* at a stated sum per day or week.

The hotel omnibus meets every train, and porters are at hand on the arrival of the company's steamers.

SOUTHWOLD AND NEIGHBOURHOOD
1900

Southwold Jack

ANDREW JOHN DAVIES

Anyone who scoffs at the idea of love at first sight should simply be packed off to Southwold in Suffolk. Here is an unspoiled seaside community with a massive common, a harbour, nine greens, a lighthouse, a sailors' reading room, a fine medieval church, wonderful domestic architecture plus many hotels, restaurants and pubs.

A veritable heaven on earth – and anyone who visits Southwold and does not immediately want to return (although I have yet to meet such an idiot) deserves both pity and censure. The rest of us form a kind of Southwold freemasonry.

What gives Southwold its unique character? First of all, there is only one road in and out, making the town virtually an island: in other words relative lack of accessibility has clearly deterred developers. Its little railway line was closed in 1929. Secondly, Southwold was devastated by its own great fire in 1659, and when the town was rebuilt, several greens were specially laid out as fire-breaks in order to reduce the possibility of future conflagration.

Thirdly, everyone who come to Southwold suddenly seems to behave better towards their fellow human beings. Businessmen who snarl and spit at work come here for a rest and unexpectedly find themselves kissing babies and saying 'Good morning' to complete strangers. Motorists give way at crossroads, while day-trippers carefully put their fish and chip wrappers in the bins provided.

Finally Adnams the brewers provide the town with a useful and regular source of employment and their dray horses still plod around the streets each day, making deliveries. Like many towns, Southwold has had its own brewery since the Middle Ages but it was the arrival of George and Ernest Adnams from Berkshire in 1872 which really brought success.

People often look at the Adnams logo – a medieval foot soldier holding a sword, ready to clunk a bell – and wonder what on earth he is doing there. The answer is to visit St Edmund's church, completed in 1460 and displaying the flint and hammerbeam roof which characterizes so many East Anglian churches.

Walk inside and immediately in front of you is the wooden figure of 'Southwold Jack' who for many years has struck his bell at the start of each service, as well as welcoming brides on their wedding day. This brightly coloured little chap dates from the fifteenth century and is so lifelike that you can even make out his blood-flecked eyes and five o'clock shadow.

Mind you, the only problem with extolling the pleasures of Southwold is the selfish fear that the world and his wife will suddenly descend in force.

So, for those of you who don't know Southwold, it really isn't worth visiting. I strongly advise you to stay away. Those of you who do know Southwold – see you there next year.

THE INDEPENDENT
1995

Oh, We Do Like to Thieve Beside the Seaside

CAL McCRYSTAL

Southwold, perched on the pebbly eastern edge of England, is a worried town. Its mayor says quite simply that she is 'terrified'.

It seems only natural that, having escaped the Black Death and other pestilences that befell most English seaports in earlier times, Southwold should rail against a modern plague visiting its comfortable houses, upsetting its affluent citizens and creating in its tiny constabulary an unaccustomed watchfulness.

The mayor says, 'Southwold is a place where if you put a dog with a blue rosette up for election, people would vote for it. It's a true blue town, peaceful and law-abiding. Now this! We're frightened!'

She hands me the minutes of the last town council meeting which said that a councillor had expressed grave concern about the recent increase in crime in Southwold. He had also proposed that the clerk write to the Waveney District Council's housing officer about council tenants with known criminal tendencies being moved to an area where there were so many targets.

The WDC is based at Lowestoft which is Labour controlled and has a homelessness problem. Lowestoft is a busy container port with rougher people than one normally encounters in Southwold, a staid resort whose single fish and chip shop finds it worthwhile to open for only two hours daily.

Waveney council is the authority responsible for housing those who need homes in North Suffolk. Southwold wants the 'undesirables' banned and a police vetting for traces of 'criminality'. It wants Southwold to remain unsullied, its nineteenth-century inshore lighthouse a shining beacon for an inward-looking community rather than for human wreckage beyond.

Could it be snobbery? 'Oh no!' says the mayor. 'We all mix well together. I have a humble background.'

The councillor who raised the alarm about criminal incomers says, 'There have been between fifty and sixty incidents of crime lately. Everyone is getting exceedingly cheesed off. We don't expect everything to be 100 per cent, but Waveney has moved people in here who have criminal backgrounds. I am trying to protect our residents.'

The town seems at ease with itself, the streets almost empty. In the Swan Hotel, backing onto Adnams' brewery, there are tweeds and cravats and silver-knobbed canes. In the Crown Hotel genteel accents tinkle among the coffee spoons. Around oaken tables are impregnable self-satisfaction and antique reminiscence.

On the seafront stands the Southwold Sailors' Reading Room, built in 1864 by the widow of a sailor lost at sea and maintained since then by a succession of philanthropists and by casual donations. There are pictures on the walls: bearded old salts from another era when fisherfolk wore the spirit of hardy England on their faces. An old man points to holes in the panelling. 'That's where the donation box was,' he says. 'They broke in last night and stole it, the fourth time in the past month.'

He nods at a broken 'porthole' in a door leading to the recreation room. 'They tried there too. They've done the British Legion and the Golf Club as well. The police cars can't catch the miscreants.'

A booklet, *Discovering Southwold*, refers to the 'complex pattern of streets and greens which . . . have a unique, elusive magic'. They confuse at

Centre Cliff in 1898 showing the Sailors' Reading Room on the left and fishing boats on the beach.

first, but within a couple of hours one understands how 'miscreants' might safely slip away to the small terraces beside Might's Creek on the marshes – council houses.

The Mayor says, 'About a month ago, in the space of a week, almost every public hall was broken into – the United Reform church, the Church of England, the Conservative Club, small lock-up businesses on the harbour, the ice cream kiosk. Some privately owned beach huts on the front were vandalized.'

A Neighbourhood Watch scheme has been set up, an unwelcome concession to alien encroachment into what a guidebook describes as a 'law-abiding populace'. The Mayor is the Neighbourhood Watch coordinator. 'Until two years ago nobody locked their doors. But in one night, a month ago, we had four burglaries in my road.'

Most of medieval Southwold was destroyed in a fire in 1659, and was declared a 'disaster area' by Parliament. A nationwide collection helped to rebuild it, and it flourished thanks to the herring fleet and the gentry who made it a favourite watering place. Grand buildings rose. In one of the Georgian houses the young George Orwell stayed occasionally with his parents, disliking Southwold intensely. The local historical society responds by disliking the house's 'nasty double glazing'. Today, the mayor insists, there are hardly any *nouveaux riches*.

The poor live in the street just before the bridge, some of them in council houses. One says that Southwold has been a 'safe little haven' for her children but 'it's a very snobby place'. She says it took two years before the council allowed a launderette to open on the High Street, for the benefit of the caravanners at the harbour.

Down the street an ambulance has drawn up to take a child to hospital. The father arrives, discouraging conversation with an angry gesture. The police are not in evidence.

Like the fish and chip shop Southwold's police station opens for business two hours a day. But in Lowestoft a police spokesman dismisses the suggested vetting of the Southwold-bound. And Waveney's housing chairman says the town's proposed ban is 'disgraceful'.

Slowly but surely Southwold is being swept into modern England.

THE INDEPENDENT ON SUNDAY

1991

Maggs About Southwold

James Maggs of Southwold (1797–1890), schoolmaster, auctioneer and general factotum, was ideally placed to know practically everything that happened in the little Suffolk port. From 1818–71 he kept a chronicle of local events, recording with scrupulous accuracy the fortunes and – more often – misfortunes of the seafarers, small tradesmen and others who were his fellow townsmen.

'Limping Gem' was both discreet and objective, well trusted and the friend of many. Such, however, was his innate curiosity and eye for detail, particularly when either the past or present of Southwold and its neighbourhood was involved, that he could not fail to tell us more than was intended both about the place and about the nineteenth century in coastal and rural Suffolk. Maggs compiled, albeit unwittingly, an important social document.

1823. Dec 6. Self [Maggs] elected Coroner for this Borough in the place of Mr. Charles Covell, resigned . . .

1823. Dec 28. Mr. Henry Oldring of this Town, Twine Spinner, on his way to Leiston, was accidentally shot by a Gamekeeper so dreadfully in the face that totally perished the sight of one eye.

1824. Oct 25. I went to Benhall respecting the following melancholy accident. On Sunday the 24. inst. a person was discovered in a well near some cottages, and upon taking it out it was found to be the body of Mr. John Banks of the Blue Anchor public house, Walberswick. The deceased had been to Wickham Market and from not having been seen or heard of since the evening of the Thursday previous, no doubt but it was when the accident occured. As it also appeared in evidence to the inquest that a noise was observed in the evening of Thursday by the rattling of the well gear but thought nothing of, and also on this same evening his speaking to a person near Benhall he should call at a cottage close by. Near to this cottage was the well and adjoining it a stile. And no doubt from the darkness of the evening he mistook the well for the stile and was the cause of this melancholy catastrophe.

1824. Dec 5. Two chimney sweeps – Isaac Foulsham and Middleton – were lodged in this jail charged of having robbed Mr. Willm Leatherdale of Reydon and a Mrs. Cooper in this town of several articles from their dwelling houses. The 8th they were committed to Ipswich for trial. At Bury Assizes both transported for 14 years.

1825. Small Pox raging here. An almost general inoculation. Some few families approved of Vaccination. Only five deaths. Minors.

1827. Augt 6. Mr. Wm Watson who on being upon a visit to this town was amusing himself at the harbour by sending his dog into the sea and fearing the dog would be drowned, attempted to save him, was unfortunately drowned himself.

1827. Oct 31 and Nov 1. An extraordinary high tide – upwards of four acres of arable land from the Easton Farm were swept entirely away by the sea from 10 to 12 feet in breadth. Taking the entire length was carried away from off Gun Hill and so undermined that large masses of earth were for days caving down. The walk from Gun Hill to New York Cliff lost from 6 to 7 feet in width and a path was obliged to be taken off the lawn in front of the lodging house, the property of the Barber's. A boathouse used by the Preventive Service standing upon the beach near New York Cliff was entirely swept away. Also a clamp of bricks and shed in a marsh, the property of Mr. Saml Laws being from 6 to 7 feet in the Jetty Road marshes.

1832. May 26. We were visited with an awful thunderstorm. A ball of electric fluid fell on Gun Hill where it spent itself in 5 different zig-zag directions, leaving its parched traces on the grass for days and in so regular a form – had they been laid out by scale and compass could not have been more exact.

1832. Oct 24. A bet was decided between Mr John Cottingham and Mr. Robert Bird – the former bets the latter that he could not walk from Southwold to Dunwich in One hour and half. Mr. B performed the task in 47 and a half min. Mr Jonthn Gooding: Umpire. Mr. C was disappointed.

He expected Mr. B would have cross'd the river in a ferry-boat, then he would not have walked the distance. But Mr. Bird had a range of boats placed across the river forming a bridge!

March 31st Sunday. The banns of marriage between Wm Wright of this town, blacksmith, and Sarah Skoulding were published by the Rev. Mr. Birch of this church and openly Forbidden by the father of the latter which the clergyman signified to the congregation.

1840. June 18th. A Mr. Bradfield assuming a Surgeon was here on a visit at Dr. Wake's and gave lecture upon anatomy, showing the wisdom of the creator, etc. July 24. Mr. B gave at the Town Hall gratuitous a lecture upon the Natural History of Man and the intellectual abilities of the negro, and on the 30th a lecture upon Phrenology. In the month of August following Mr. B left Southwold to reside at Halesworth where he continued 'till the ensuing Michlmas when to the great annoyance of the tradesmen at Halesworth, Southwold, Beccles and Norwich he turned out nothing more or less than a downright Swindler. He was after some little pains apprehended and lodged in Newgate where no doubt he received many more lectures than he gave the Southwolders. During his stay here he published a 'Treatise on Bathing' at the expense of Mr. Tippell, Halesworth, Printer.

1844. Feby 28th. Mr. Boyce aged 78 was found in a hay loft the property of Mr. Edwd Freeman hanging. The last time the deceased was seen alive was about One PM on the 26th inst. He was on the point of marriage to a Mrs. George of Ringsfield – his banns were published the last time on the Sunday 25th. March 1st Inquest was held. Verdict Insanity. Deceased for many years had been Constable, High Constable, Assistant Overseer.

1845. Novr 12. Wednesday evening between 6 and 7 o'clock a cottage the property of Mr. Jas Lincoln in Pinkney's Lane was discovered to be on fire. But soon got under without much damage. Presently after it was announced that Mr. Lincoln, shoemaker, and Mr. Geo Mayes, watchmaker, had had their houses robbed, the former of one sovereign and the latter of 10 and a half. Two women of this town were suspected, named 'Bugg' and 'Cotton', but could not be proved agt them. But however on the following day such circumstantial evidences came before the Magistrates as inclined everyone to suppose the wife of Mr. Mayes was the guilty party and fired the house (tho' hard to say) to blind the robbery. Being only circumstantial evidence the enquiry ceased.

1850. Oct 20. This morning and until about 11 o'clock strong wind from the N.E. About 11 the wind abated when a large shoal of herrings were observed in the bay. Boats and nets were immediately in request and I witnessed that in the course of 4 or 5 hours £100's worth of Herring were landed. There would have been more had the boats been larger, as the Nets so soon as cast into the sea sank with the quantity of fish. This was as an old woman observed a 'lucky Godsend'.

THE SOUTHWOLD DIARY OF JAMES MAGGS, 1818–1876
THE SUFFOLK RECORDS SOCIETY, 1984

Fanny Foster

MARGOT STRICKLAND

Georgiana Fanny Julia Foster was born at Thorpe St Andrew outside Norwich on 11 October 1891. When she was a few years old the family came to live at Southwold in one of the pretty houses overlooking Sole Bay. Before it lay a smooth greensward on which ladies in long skirts and gentlemen in panama hats could be seen striking coloured wooden balls through hoops with mallets. For in Southwold in those days, croquet was a favourite pastime.

When the St Felix school for girls was projected Fanny's mother was appointed one of the governors and when Fanny was old enough it was inevitable that she should join the school – and taken every day by horse and cart with other girls.

She was a clever girl for whom a brilliant future was predicted. She loved Latin and music and learned to play the violin, practising every morning for three quarters of an hour before breakfast. In the school holidays and at weekends she often wore her favourite clothes, a red coat and hat, but she disliked intensely the black buttoned boots that girls wore at the turn of the century.

Severe storms lashed the East Anglian coast in 1905 and the smooth green croquet lawn in front of the house was swept away by huge waves. This event presaged a change in the lives of Fanny and her mother, for her father died. Now relatively poor they moved to a house in Park Lane formerly occupied by Agnes Strickland, the historian and author of *The Queens of England*.

At St Felix Fanny had one thought in mind – to become educated. And she had a passion for learning. It was not difficult to find a place at the new women's college at Oxford and Cambridge so she begged her mother to let her have a university career. She went up to Newnham College, Cambridge, in 1910.

In those golden days before the First World War life for the undergraduate at Cambridge was idyllic. There was clever conversation with like minds, about science, and music, letters, art and drama. But after three years Fanny went home to care for her mother who was ailing. Now she reverted to the 'daughter at home' existence which blighted the lives of so many young women. Her brain, however, could not long remain idle.

She began a series of correspondence courses, learning photography, acquiring a reflex camera, dishes, chemicals and an enlarger, and with the help of Southwold's master photographer, Frederick Jenkins, set up her own dark room.

The Balkans, and especially Yugoslavia, also became a part of her life. At the end of the war British families were asked to take children from several war-torn countries into their homes, and a boy from Yugoslavia arrived in Southwold. Fanny's sympathy for his plight drew him out. He talked of his

The Southwold-to-Walberswick ferry.

home and his country's customs. He learned to speak English and Fanny picked up the rudiments of Serbo-Croat. Now she began her most important and intense studies. She taught herself the language with the aid of a dictionary and mastered it.

Fanny looked after her mother for sixteen years and on her death in 1922 she was at last free. An uncle bequeathed her an income for life, and she decided to travel. In 1924 she took a cargo boat bound for New Zealand taking with her a pair of field glasses, a Thurston Dalmeyer Reflex camera with a telephoto lens, an ancient folding pocket Kodak, a tripod, dishes and chemicals.

Off the Canary Islands the ship grounded on rocks and she took to the lifeboats. And on the second leg of the journey she befriended one of the ship's officers, James Blake, and romance blossomed. A few years younger than Fanny he fell desperately in love with her and implored her to marry him. She felt she could not do this, but she agreed to let him write to her.

Back in Southwold life could never be the same again. James Blake continued to write affectionate letters, but within two years he had suffered heatstroke while off Port Sudan, died, and was buried at sea. All that remained of the one love of Fanny's life was a small packet of letters tied with blue ribbon.

Fanny's knowledge of Serbo-Croat came to the notice of the Yugoslavian government and she was awarded the first of several travelling scholarships. It was highly unusual for an English woman with a good knowledge of the language and literature of the country to visit Belgrade and she was lionized wherever she went. She was appointed official photographer for two archaeological expeditions, translated volumes of Serbo-Croatian poetry and other works, and in 1937 she was presented to King Peter II who conferred on her the Order of St Sava. This medal is in the Southwold museum.

She was now closely involved in the local community but with the outbreak of the Second World War she went to London to work in a department linked with Eastern Europe. After the war she met President Tito in London.

But Southwold now took over her life and she devoted her energies to doing good by stealth. Her advice was sought by many on matters of every kind. She was a familiar figure about the town, usually dressed in sombre colours, though she occasionally surprised her friends by making an appearance in the favourite colour of her youth – scarlet. She had learned to drive and would rush about in a green Baby Austin car. A regular churchgoer, she liked a pew to herself. If anybody tried to join her she would grope about on the floor pretending to get her Bible out of a box until they went away.

She was not domesticated and boasted that she had never once made her own bed. This task was performed by Mrs Upcraft who cleaned and cooked for her for thirty-five years. It was said that when her ancient toaster burnt the toast one day she took both the toast and the toaster to the electrician and asked for it to be repaired.

Fanny loved cats and dogs, in that order, knew the names of most of the ones in Southwold and on her royal progress around the greens and streets she would always stop and talk to any she saw.

The conservation of Southwold, constantly under threat of development, became her passion. She abhorred all things modern. It was said of her that she considered 'Southwold, first, last and all the time'. She was on all the local and country planning and housing committees.

Fanny was regarded with a mixture of affection and awe by most of the people of Southwold. She was unpopular with those who sought to modernize the town and its amenities and make it a profitable and popular resort. She fought them. Once when walking, a friend drew her out of the path of a lorry. 'You don't want to get run over, do you?' the friend said. Fanny looked critically at the lorry which should not have been on the road and replied 'For a principle, yes'.

She owned several properties and refused to make money out of them – selling them for absurdly small sums and never allowing them to be sold to outsiders as holiday cottages. She served on Southwold Borough Council for thirty-two years and was elected mayor three times. A new housing development was named for her – Foster Close.

One of her admirers was a wandering minstrel who, knowing her love of music, serenaded her with his violin beneath her window. She usually gave him a meal before he went off to spend the night at the workhouse at Blythburgh.

At the age of eighty-three she was found one day lying unconscious in the street. A boy riding a bicycle had accidentally knocked her over. She refused to give his name and died the following year after never fully recovering.

St Edmund's church was crowded with people and flowers for her memorial service. A plaque subscribed for by the people of Southwold was put up alongside one in memory of her father in the chancel. All the mourners spoke fondly of this legend about whom tales were legion.

Some years earlier Reg Carter, the Southwold cartoonist, did a sketch that appeared in a shop window in the High Street. A man asks the unmistakably dumpy figure of Fanny Foster, 'And how do you like Southwold?'

Fanny replies, 'I am Southwold.'

It was said that Fanny had stood on the steps of the Town Hall and spoken those very words for all to hear. And if Fanny Foster was Southwold she was also England.

I AM SOUTHWOLD
1983

A Bracing Dip in Majorville

GERALDINE BEDELL

Majorism has made it into the *Shorter Oxford English Dictionary* so now everyone wants to know what it is. The *Independent* has invited readers to send in suggestions: reporters have been dispatched to Brixton to see if they can spot it. But I can tell them that they are looking in the wrong place.

I discovered Southwold last week and I shall be back this bank holiday, basking in Majorism. Southwold is a seaside resort which stopped in 1962 before sexual intercourse began. In Southwold children play purposefully on the beach with buckets and spades, in knickers and cardigans, while their parents huddle cheerfully behind windbreaks or brew tea in beach huts. When you undress for your dip in the sludgey brown sea, you do it beneath a homemade towelling beach robe with an elasticated neck.

Southwold is time travel in Suffolk: a town of warm beer and cold sea, where mums, dads and children walk along the front in the evening, the Methodist Hall offers improving talks on local history, and householders fly Union Jacks in their front gardens. It is not twee, nor is it tainted by ghetto-blasters, louts or post-modern confusions.

It is a place of utter respectability, run according to lower-middle class values of self-improvement and not annoying your neighbours.

For me it is a return to blissful childhood. It is where John Major should be holidaying, rather than letting down Majorists by fleeing to a villa in Portugal. He would have been perfect as the Mayor of Southwold.

INDEPENDENT ON SUNDAY

1993

February

LEONORA STARR

The morning was so perfect that my heart went soaring with the larks. A cloudless sky, a sea of turquoise silk whose edges ruffle gently on pale sands, no breath of wind to stir the elms, their twigs already flushed with rising sap.

A day too rare and precious to be spent indoors and so, abandoning all that should be done, I set forth with the dogs across The Common.

One never knows what will lie between home and the horizon. Sometimes it is as though the east winds drained the land of life, so that it is unfriendly in its bleakness. Sometimes the countryside beyond the Blyth is brightly coloured, the pines of Blythburgh heronry richly green, the bracken on Walberswick common emerald or rusty gold according to the season, marsh pools flashing in the sun, tiled roofs orange and pink and rippling black, the ancient tower of Blythburgh standing high above the marshes it has guarded for so many centuries.

From Southwold this morning it was though a veil of soft blue gauze had fallen beyond the river, blurring the landscape so that only known shapes might be guessed and found. To any stranger it must remain a hyacinth mystery.

It was on such a morning as today, ten years ago, that on the road across the marsh to Blackshore a curious experience befell me. It was noon on a

Beach huts north of the pier.

bright February day. On either side of the straight road lay brimming dikes, beyond them open marshes, and ahead the Blackshore cottages clustered by the river.

I had been following a heron's flight across the marsh when, looking once more ahead, I saw a funeral party. Men and women, eight or nine of them and all in black, were gathered about a hand bier on which a coffin rested. They were walking towards me, obviously on a sad journey to the churchyard.

Since they were already a considerable distance from the cottages it seemed strange I had not seen them until now, but to this I gave no thought, being concerned lest the cairns of that day, Becky and her son Hamish, should bark in an unseemly manner. I called them back. For once they were obedient, and I stopped to put them on their leads, a matter of less than a minute.

When I stood upright again the road was empty, not a human being in sight. There was no side road, not a bush or a haystack nor any other sort of cover. No one, I later found upon inquiry, had died at Blackshore for some considerable time.

I am no judge of distances, but I made note of exactly where the funeral procession had been when first I saw it, and of my own position, and William later judged the distance to be 40 yards. I can discover no talk of any ghostly happenings on that road, nor can I hear of anyone who has seen a similar funeral party. What had become of it I have no idea to this day.

Southwold, however, does not lack for ghostly stories. There is the old lady who is said to walk on Skilman's Hill with her little dog, though I have never seen her nor met anyone who had.

There is the headless soldier of Gun Hill who has been seen on moonlight nights by an elderly lady who assures me that in her young days it was no unusual event for him to be seen standing by the second cannon as one approached from South Green, yet I have never heard of his appearance in the five-and-twenty years I have known the town. Is this because the psychic waves or whatever it may be that enables mortal eyes to see the supernatural grow gradually weaker in the course of time? Or is it that the present generation are less receptive to such influences than those of former days?

The guns in question are six old cannon that if tradition is to be believed were given to Southwold by the Duke of Cumberland on his way south from Culloden where he had captured them from the Young Pretender, who had taken them from Sir John Cope on the field of Preston. The Duke was said to have given them to the people of Southwold out of gratitude for the warm welcome given to him when he landed there owing to the stress of weather – although another version has it that they caused his ship to roll so that he was only too thankful to be rid of them!

During the war they were taken from their wooden mountings, removed from their position on a low cliff pointing out to sea, and laid low among the long grass beneath neighbouring trees for fear the sight of them from the

St James Green in winter.

air might cause the enemy to classify Southwold as a fortified town, and bomb it accordingly.

The Council has decreed that as soon as wood may be obtained for the replacement of the former mountings, now rotted beyond further use, the old guns shall be reinstated on Gun Hill.

When that day comes it will be interesting to see whether the soldier – if he reappears – will take up his position as before. The second gun might well be given some other place, and if that happens will he change his stance?

Is it the gun he haunts or that particular position? Probably the gun, for the tale goes that he (literally!) lost his head on an occasion when it failed to fire. He, searching for the reason of failure, somewhat rashly looked down the muzzle. The gun at that unlikely moment fired and he became a headless ghost.

Sutherland House, opposite the post office, was haunted during the occupation of a former owner by a charming apparition, although the present occupants have no belief in her existence. (It was in this house that James II, then Duke of York, kept his naval headquarters in the wars against the Dutch.) The haunting experienced consisted of light footsteps coming at night down from the top floor to the first floor where the former owner slept. A gentle hand smoothed the bedclothes up about his shoulders and adjusted the eiderdown if it threatened to slide off in the tiresome fashion of most eiderdowns. A kindly spirit!

Once, years ago, as I was passing by, I saw a young girl looking from an upper window. I judged her to be sixteen or seventeen. Chestnut hair hung to her shoulders from a centre parting, an unusual fashion for that time, though recently it has become ordinary enough. She wore a gown of blue material resembling taffetas, full-skirted, the bodice low and closely fitting with a white ruffle at her bosom. She leaned her head against one arm that reached above her, holding to the curtain.

Yet though her appearance and dress were far from usual it was the radiance and serenity of her expression that impressed her in my memory, so that I see her now as clearly as twelve years ago, lips parted in a smile, happy eyes blue as her dress, and bright with interest as she stood there looking down into the street.

A few days later I made some remark concerning her to the owner when on a visit to his antique shop on the ground floor. Strangely he looked at me, asked at which window she had been standing, shook his head with a half-smile and a sigh. 'I've never seen her, and I don't suppose I ever shall. The door of that room has been locked for weeks, and no one but myself has even been upstairs.'

Recently the old house passed into new hands and has been restored with intelligence and skill in such a manner as to emphasise its character to the best advantage. In the course of reconstruction Tudor windows were discovered behind the plaster, and huge fireplaces disclosed behind Victorian grates.

The new owners are most fortunately people of discernment. They run it as a restaurant. We are lucky in having one so much in keeping with the character of this little town – a character that may be all too soon lost among so-called improvements such as concrete edges to the ancient greens, cafeterias, kiosks, swimming pools and concrete bathing huts in place of the old wooden ones painted pink and blue that used to lend the beach such gaiety and charm.

TO PLEASE MYSELF

1948

The Last Laugh

MAUREEN LIPMAN

Earlier this year the BBC Holiday programme sent me to Las Vegas, along with the great and near great. They were so pleased with the results, they invited me to go on holiday again. This time it was to Southwold. With my mother. The only thing the two programmes will have in common is that they're both a bit of a gamble.

Still, I do love Southwold. It's often painted as the town that time forgot, but its memory has lingered on with me since I first saw it seven years ago. Rows of brightly painted bathing huts, an unchanging harbour, the colours not of Hockney but of Turner, a proudly named 'ferry' consisting of old Bob in his rowing boat, a sedate market place and a Norman church big enough for most of Suffolk to worship in.

'I wish you people would stop coming down here, trying to put us on the map,' snapped a tweedy resident at the first sight of our sound boom. 'I don't suppose it occurs to you that there's simply nowhere to park at weekends, now that you lot keep endlessly going on about how unspoilt we are!'

Well, sorry ma'am but you are, and though we haven't come on a spoiling mission, I have, in my task as a roving recommender, to report that the air was clean (always excepting the Sizewell signs to mar one's approach), the natives friendly and the pace sedate. The town is lively with binoculared visitors, bustling with bistros and after twenty-four hours I felt better than I had in weeks.

'So you like it here,' I prompted Mum as we walked, microphones down our bras and cameramen backing down the street before us, towards the sea front.

'Oh, it's fabulous,' she beamed, 'what a wonderful spot. Who'd have thought it? I mean I've never heard of it before . . . and isn't it clean!' (Mum's greatest accolade, a sort of Egon Lipman, highly polished, five stars.) 'You could eat off the streets – and isn't The Swan marvellous! It's like a five-star hotel, there's nothing you could want for. I mean it's so refined and . . . well, I couldn't fault the place really, it's beautiful.'

'It is,' I nodded, then I added, probingly for the viewers' benefit, 'so, you would come here with a friend for a weekend?'

She looked at me as though I'd suggested throwing a bar mitzvah in the Vatican. 'Me come here? Noooo! What would I do? I'd be bored stiff.'

My eyes were jitterbugging signals at her. I felt like a lighthouse. But Mum was blissfully unaware that this was perhaps not the way to 'present' to camera. Maybe her approach was a healthy one. Certainly it might make for funnier viewing. I can't imagine Judith Chalmers wishing she wasn't here in quite the way Mum did. 'Cut!' said John, the director.

Later he had arranged to film the town crier welcoming us into Southwold in traditional fashion. In full regalia and facial fuzz, he rang his bell, 'Oyezed' thrice, unrolled his scroll and in a barnstorming baritone which made Brian Blessed sound like Blossom Dearie, boomed, 'We are proud to welcome Miss Maureen Lipman and her mother Zemla to Southwold.' Mother and daughter fell off their bench, John called 'Cut!' yet again and pointed out politely that although Zelma was an unusual name it's better to say it correctly, since Zemla sounded like a baby tiger cub in Whipsnade or something you rub on your bunions.

Three days fled past. We ate well, the sun shone, I bought a watercolour of bluebells in one of the many local galleries, we laughed a lot, no one more than the person who caused the laughter, and we came home refreshed and replete.

On the quayside I bought fresh-today fish from an extraordinarily chic fishmonger, to butter up my fish-loving husband. I seemed to buy forty quids worth of London fish for £18. You could have knocked me down with a wet turbot. Perhaps that's why they call it the town that time forgot.

GOOD HOUSEKEEPING
1994

Southwold Museum Curator Replies to Criticism

GEORGE BUMSTEAD

I feel I must take issue with Ms Lipman who asked in the BBC programme *Holiday*, 'what attracts people to a place with no attractions?'

First of all life in Southwold does not revolve around beach huts. Any owner will tell you that they are more trouble than they are worth. And people do not sit in them all day gazing at what is recognized as being the most inhospitable sea in the world.

I have to say to Ms Lipman that all the things we haven't got which you think we should have – we don't want.

And I offer you a list of what thousands of civilized visitors to Southwold find attractive, and concentrated as they are, can almost be reached on foot.

You can swim in the cleanest water on the east coast with a lifeguard in attendance.

You can play golf any time, any day.

There are two rugby pitches, a football pitch and a cricket pitch, fresh water and sea angling, sailing in ocean-going yachts, sail boarding and canoeing. You can cycle or walk miles along the old railway track, completely free of cars, and there are acres of common land for horse riding.

Southwold's annual yacht regatta.

George Bumstead in his much-loved grocery shop shortly before it closed in 1984, after forty years' service.

There are tennis courts, and a five-a-side and a skate board rink. There are allotments at £5 a year if you wish to grow your own.

Nowhere in Southwold is more than 25 yards from premises where you can purchase alcohol – with a brewery on the spot to top up the stocks. No one has ever been known to die of thirst in Southwold.

Even shopping is an interesting experience, rather than a necessity.

We also have a well-appointed caravan site, and an adequate site for tents – a sight cheaper than the accommodation on offer in a holiday programme on Cuba.

If you suffer from stress I would recommend a walk along the ferry path – to just watch the sheep and cattle quietly grazing on the marshes.

You seem to have a problem with what you would do after six o'clock in the evening in Southwold.

Well, we have a Wildlife Society, badminton, bridge, yoga, sequence dancing, snooker, an Art Circle, an Archaeological and Natural History Society and a Decorative and Fine Arts Society.

Also we have our very own theatre company which plays to capacity audiences for nine weeks in high season.

You gave the impression that Southwold was 100 years behind the times and not in the 'real world'.

I must take you to task on this one, Ms Lipman. We are seven miles as the seagull flies from two nuclear power stations, with yet another on the drawing board. The Pressurised Water Reactor is the first in this country and yet untried, and if anything ever goes wrong, then we in Southwold will be the first to know.

Also, until quite recently, there was an American air base just 20 miles away and before the end of the Cold War heavily armed warplanes screamed over Southwold, sometimes at roof top level – and as they still do from time to time.

Finally, Ms Lipman, the town museum has a folder containing a description of our collection in nine languages all translated by local people. If nothing else that says something about the people who live in Southwold.

LOWESTOFT JOURNAL

1994

Sources

'In the reign of King Edward VII', 'Battle of Sole Bay', 'A Health Resort' and 'Grand Hotel', from *Southwold and Neighbourhood*, 1900.

'Far Away Places have nothing on Southwold', Miles Kington, *Ms London*, 1982, by kind permission of the author.

'Swallows', Daniel Defoe, from *Tour Through the Eastern Counties*, 1724.

'A Day out like your Mother used to make', Steve Boggan, 1992; 'Southwold Jack', Andrew John Davies, 1995; 'Oh, We do like to thieve beside the seaside', Cal McCrystal, 1992, and 'A Bracing Dip in Majorville', Geraldine Bedall, 1993; all by kind permission of *Independent* Newspaper Publishing.

'Once an Village, now a Town Corporate', Thomas Gardner, from *A Historical Account of Dunwich, Blithburgh and Southwold*, 1754.

'Southwold Fashioned', Christopher Matthew, 1987, by kind permission of *Punch* Ltd.

'A Sea-washed Town', 'Birds of 1838' and 'Hints to Sea-Bathers', by Robert Wake, from *Southwold and Its Vicinity*, 1838.

'Inns of Happiness', David Gibbs, 1992, by kind permission of the *Brisbane Courier Mail*, Australia.

'Discovering Southwold', Alan Bottomley, 1986, by kind permission of the Southwold and Reydon Society and the Suffolk Preservation Society.

'Local Hero', Terry Reeve, 1997, by kind permission of the *Lowestoft Journal*.

'Sunny Periods in Southwold' is taken from *East Anglia* by Peter Sager, translated by David Henry Wilson, Pallas Athene, London, 2nd edn, 1996

'The Royal Camp', '1984' and 'Fanny Foster', Margot Strickland, 1983, by kind permission of the author.

'Southwold's Magical Christmas', John Miller, 1997, from the Southwold Christmas Lights official programme.

'June' and 'February 1947', from *To Please Myself*, 1947, Leonora Starr, by kind permission of Dr Piers Mackesy.

'War Years 1939–45', from *Story of Southwold*, 1956, J.S. Hurst, by kind permission of Ann Thornton.

'From Now on Home is where the Hut is', Rohan Daft, 1994, by kind permission of the *Evening Standard*.

'Shrimps and Golf', Richard Sisley, 1893, from the *Pall Mall Magazine*.

'Into Eden, East of Ipswich', Byron Rogers, 1995, by kind permission of the *Sunday Telegraph*.

'Pride of the Ages', Arthur Mee, 1941, from *The King's England* series, Suffolk.

'The Southwold Railway', J.D. Mann, 1996, by kind permission of *Suffolk Life*.

'Maggs about Southwold', from the *Southwold Diary of James Maggs 1818–1896*, edited by Alan Bottomley, 1984, by kind permission of the Suffolk Records Society, and Helen Surtees.

'The Last Laugh', Maureen Lipman, 1994, by kind permission of the author and the *Good Housekeeping* helpline.

'Museum Curator Replies to Criticism', George Bumstead, 1994, by kind permission of the author.

Picture Credits

Southwold Town Council: pages xii, 2, 3, 12, 13, 19, 20, 25, 35, 40, 52, 68, 85, 92; Southwold Archaeological and Natural History Society Museum: pages 21, 24; Stephen Wolfenden: pages 7, 29, 38, 71, 80, 99, 111, 112; Richard Wells: pages ii, 9, 16, 44, 48, 54, 57, 60, 66, 70, 87, 105, 106.

ABOUT THE EDITOR

John Miller moved from London to Southwold – where he lives in the High Street with his wife and two cats – in 1987, after spending much of his working life with the *Daily Telegraph* as a foreign correspondent and Kremlinologist. He serves on the Town Council and is a member of several local societies. He golfs enthusiastically on The Common, likes to spend the summer in the family beach hut, and just *occasionally* swims in the sea. He says, 'When I die and go to heaven it will be an anticlimax after living in Southwold.'